McCARTNEY
20 Years on His Own

By Edward Gross

PIONEER BOOKS, INC.   LAS VEGAS, NEVADA

Designed and Edited by Hal Schuster

OTHER PIONEER BOOKS

•THE MAGICAL MICHAEL JACKSON
Edited by Hal Schuster. March, 1990. $9.95, ISBN#1-55698-235-6
•FISTS OF FURY: THE FILMS OF BRUCE LEE
Written by Edward Gross. March, 1990. $14.95, ISBN #1-55698-233-X
•WHO WAS THAT MASKED MAN?
Written by James Van Hise. March, 1990. $14.95, ISBN #1-55698-227-5
•PAUL MCCARTNEY: 20 YEARS ON HIS OWN
Written by Edward Gross. February, 1990. $9.95, ISBN #1-55698-263-1
•THE DARK SHADOWS TRIBUTE BOOK
Written by Edward Gross and James Van Hise. February, 1990. $14.95, ISBN#1-55698-234-8
•THE UNOFFICIAL TALE OF BEAUTY AND THE BEAST, 2nd Edition
Written by Edward Gross. $14.95, 164 pages, ISBN #1-55698-261-5
•TREK: THE LOST YEARS
Written by Edward Gross. $12.95, 128 pages, ISBN #1-55698-220-8
•THE TREK ENCYCLOPEDIA
Written by John Peel. $19.95, 368 pages, ISBN#1-55698-205-4
•HOW TO DRAW ART FOR COMIC BOOKS
Written by James Van Hise. $14.95, 160 pages, ISBN#1-55698-254-2
•THE TREK CREW BOOK
Written by James Van Hise. $9.95, 112 pages, ISBN#1-55698-256-9
•THE OFFICIAL PHANTOM SUNDAYS
Written by Lee Falk. $14.95, 128 pages, ISBN#1-55698-250-X
•BLONDIE & DAGWOOD: AMERICA'S FAVORITE FAMILY
Written by Dean Young. $6.95, 132 pages, ISBN#1-55698-222-4
•THE DOCTOR AND THE ENTERPRISE
Written by Jean Airey. $9.95, 136 pages, ISBN#1-55698-218-6
•THE MAKING OF THE NEXT GENERATION
Written by Edward Gross. $14.95, 128 pages, ISBN#1-55698-219-4
•THE MANDRAKE SUNDAYS
Written by Lee Falk. $12.95, 104 pages, ISBN#1-55698-216-X
•BATMANIA
Written by James Van Hise. $14.95, 176 pages, ISBN#1-55698-252-6
•GUNSMOKE
Written by John Peel. $14.95, 204 pages, ISBN#1-55698-221-6
•ELVIS-THE MOVIES: THE MAGIC LIVES ON
Written by Hal Schuster. $14.95, ISBN#1-55698-223-2
•STILL ODD AFTER ALL THESE YEARS: ODD COUPLE COMPANION.
Written by Edward Gross. $12.95, 132 pages, ISBN#1-55698-224-0
•SECRET FILE: THE UNOFFICIAL MAKING OF A WISEGUY
Written by Edward Gross. $14.95, 164 pages, ISBN#1-55698-261-5

Library of Congress Cataloging-in-Publication Data
Edward Gross, 1960—
    McCartney: 20 Years on His Own

    1.   McCartney: 20 Years on His Own (music)
I. Title

Published by Pioneer Books, Inc., 5715 N. Balsam Rd., Las Vegas, NV, 89130.

First Printing, 1990

TO KAREN WRITER
BEATLE BUDDY TO THE END

AUTHOR'S NOTE: Over the past twenty years, Paul McCartney has discussed his career with a variety of journalists, preserving for posterity's sake an in-depth and comprehensive look at his life. It is from Rolling Stone, Good Day Sunshine, Musician, Beatlefan, The Flowers in the Dirt Tour Book, Paul McCartney: The Definitive Biography, The London Times, Newsweek, The New York Times and the radio series McCartney on McCartney that many of the comments presented in this volume have been culled, in an attempt to provide an overall view of Paul McCartney's solo career. The only frustration that has arisen from such research is that journalists have consistently focused their interviews on some aspect of the Beatles, as opposed to discussing McCartney's current achievements, thus limiting the information available concerning the solo years.

For their invaluable assistance, the author would like to thank photographer Bill Last; Chris Schanke, for his audio assistance; Bill Wallgreen, for permission to reprint his reviews of McCartney bootlegs; and, especially, Charles Rosenay, the President of Liverpool Productions and publisher of Good Day Sunshine, for aid he provided through the writing of this book. A special note of thanks to my wife, Eileen, who has once again had to put up with my obsessions while I'm writing a book, and my baby son, Teddy, whose bopping to Beatle tunes ranks with the best of them.

Also a special acknowledgement to John Lennon, Paul McCartney, George Harrison and Ringo Starr—the Beatles—without whom the past twenty six years wouldn't have been the same.

COVER PHOTO BY BILL LAST

CONTENTS

INTRODUCTION: GETTING BACK

*"It's
been really nice to
get back to those songs,"
notes Paul McCartney regarding the
performance of Beatles songs during his
Flowers in the Dirt world tour, "and I think the audience likes them. You see grown men crying. There's a lot of emotion involved, because it reminds people of either a better time or when they were first courting. These songs take people back, which is obvious, but you take 'em back to a good place, which isn't so obvious."*

"Taking 'em back," or getting back to where he once belonged, is the whole purpose of Paul McCartney going on tour in 1989 and 1990. The tour marks the first time he has done so since 1976 when his Wings Over America tour took the nation by storm. That first tour was highly significant for an artist in McCartney's position. He had to prove that there was indeed life after the Beatles. When that group disbanded in 1970, many questioned where he and the other Fabs would go. The first few solo efforts of John Lennon, George Harrison and even Ringo Starr had been very well received by critics, yet McCartney's first solo recordings in the early 1970s were savagely attacked. Undoubtedly this jarred the confidence of one of history's most influential songwriters and musicians.

Slowly he began rebuilding his creativity through the albums **McCartney, Ram, Wild Life** and **Red Rose Speedway**. But it wasn't until the phenomenal success of **Band on the Run** and **Venus and Mars** that McCartney had delivered a musical miracle a second time. Both critics and public alike hailed his return. His renewed self-confidence became obvious when he took his new band, Wings, on the road. That moment of personal triumph for McCartney caused his greatest critics—including former partner John Lennon—to stop and take notice.

"I admire the way Paul started back from scratch," Lennon noted to *Playboy*, "forming a new band and playing in small dance halls, because that's what he wanted to do with the Beatles—he wanted us to go back to the dance halls and experience that again. I didn't...But I kind of admire the way he got off his pedestal—now he's back on it again, but, I mean, he did what he wanted to do."

History is repeating itself. In the 1970s it seemed winning phenomenal success twice in one lifetime took a bit of the edge off of McCartney. He no longer had to prove himself. The quality of his music began to suffer. **Wings at the Speed of Sound, London Town** and **Back to the Egg** sold well, but the music lacked the intensity and emotional push of **Band on the Run** or **Venus and Mars**. McCartney no longer had to fight.

"I hate the idea that you've got to sweat and suffer to produce something that's good," he's said. "It's unfortunate, because who wants to go around stress all the time just to aid creativity? But when it happens, it does actually seem to help. It's a drag, because the logic follows that we should all walk around even more stressed to make better albums. Who needs it? I'd rather not make albums than do that."

These words to the contrary, the "stress" that followed his arrest in Japan during January of 1980 for the illegal possession of marijuana, and subsequent ten days spent in jail, recharged him. That year's **McCartney II**, a solo endeavor, *sold*.

McCartney: 20 Years on His Own

presence they still exude twenty years after the group disbanded.

"What we did was good," McCartney accepts. "I get letters all the time from people my age saying their kids are getting into the Beatles, and I love that. One of the things I really hate is the generation gap. I love listening to real old fellas telling their stories and I'd hate to think people didn't listen to my records because I'm old. I mean, if they don't like it, fair enough, but you shouldn't rule things out before you've given them a chance. Me and John never thought we'd carry on doing pop music after we were 30, and here I am in me mid-40s about to go on tour doing rock 'n roll. I just hope my legs hold out."

Undoubtedly they will. Over the past twenty years Paul McCartney has proven his incredible tenacity, a staying power most of today's musicians lack. Twenty years from now, who will be remembered? New Kids on the Block, Bon Jovi or McCartney?

—Edward Gross

January, 1990

Then the death of John Lennon at the end of the year affected him. 1982's **Tug of War**, his best album since **Band on the Run**, was greeted by nearly unanimous raves from critics and public. Its success restarted the cycle. Each subsequent album—**Pipes of Peace, Give My Regards to Broad Street** and **Press to Play**—marked a step down in overall lyrical quality and album continuity.

McCartney himself noted the decline and tried to get back to his roots recording a collection of rock and roll oldies. It appeared only on the Russian—but highly bootlegged and imported—**Choba B CCCP (Back in USSR)**. The collection received tremendous positive attention around the world. He channeled the renewed vitality into **Flowers in the Dirt**, his strongest album since **Tug of War**. His current tour delivers a McCartney ready to use his legacy to catapult into the '90s. Both his concerts and interviews show a McCartney finally coming to grips with his musical past, embracing rather than discouraging recollections of the Beatles, and the

8

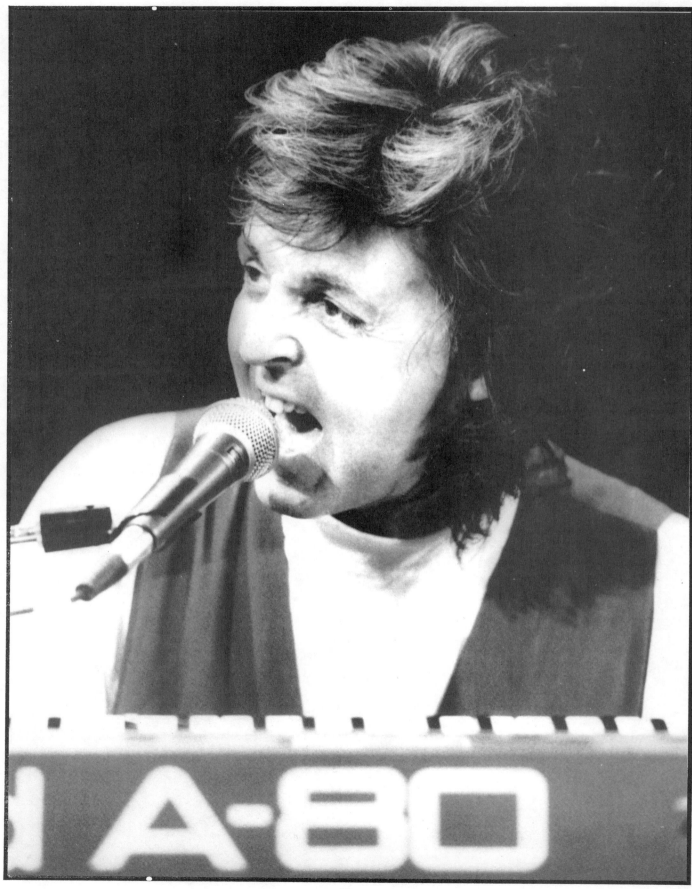

I. PAUL McCARTNEY MEETS THE PRESS

*The following edited transcript is based on three press conferences given by Paul McCartney in New York and Toronto. The first took place in August of 1989 at the Lyceum Theatre, where McCartney and his band were rehearsing for the **Flowers in the Dirt** world tour. The event began with live performances of the latest album's "Figure of Eight" and "This One," as well as a rousing rendition of 1980's "Coming Up." Then, the former Fab fielded questions for approximately an hour. The second conference took place on December 7, 1989 at Toronto's Skydome, and the third on December 12, 1989 at New York's Madison Square Garden, on the afternoon following his first appearance there since the 1976 Wings Over America tour. As has been evident since his days with the Beatles, McCartney is more than capable of handling any questions thrown his way (though he does ignore such "innocent" queries as how many women he's had in his bed at one time. "I'm not telling you," he says dryly, "especially with my wife in the same building."), displaying a quick and clever wit, completely down to Earth, despite a musical legacy that has spanned three decades.*

Q: How did this tour come about?

A: Once you've got a band that you're comfortable with, the next logical thing is to go on tour, and that's why we're doing it.

Q: Can you tell us about the band and what special ingredient each of them is bringing?

A: Starting with the drummer. I did some sessions in London, just jamming and he showed up. Each Friday night different people used to try out, various drummers, guitar players. We had quite a varied bunch of people and eventually this drummer, Chris, turned up and I liked his playing a lot and so we did some recordings with him, which turned out to be that Russian rock and roll album. Good drummer. Young guy. I like him.

Hamish Stuart, beautiful voice, good guitar player, has his own guitar and can play bass.

Linda my wife, lovely, I love her, I'm taking her on tour.

Wix, the other keyboard player, he's dealing with all the stuff that you need a degree in physics in to turn on, musical synthesizers and all that stuff.

Robbie McIntosh, excellent guitar player. And that's the band.

Q: Of all the songs you've done, how do you pick a set of songs? And currently, which one is your favorite?

A: What I did was I sat down and kind of asked myself what I would like to see him play if I was just somebody coming to the show. Or what I thought I'd like to see the band play. It came down to about 35 songs which I consider to be my best songs, and we just chose from that. Basically we chose from the rock and roll period, pre-Beatles; Beatles period; Wings period and the new album. Interesting about some of the Beatles stuff, was that I've never actually performed it on stage before. Something like "Sgt. Pepper," we only recorded. We never got to do it as the Beatles, because we'd stopped touring at that time. And I didn't realize it when I chose it, but when I got on stage, I said, "I've never done this before..." So it was very fresh for me.

Q: *Given the furor over Michael Jackson's use of "Revolution" for an advertisement, will you be accepting a corporate sponsor for your tour?*

A: The problem for me, really, is that with the Beatles we used to refuse sponsors a lot, particularly soft drinks. We could have obviously got a lot of money off that, but we tried to keep the Beatles thing very pure that way. We didn't get into a heavy commercialization of it, so I think people who like Beatles music tend not to associate it with products, they associate it with an era. They like it because it means something. I'd like it to stay that way. I think for the good of the songs it might be better that it stay that way. That's just something I need to talk to Michael about some time.

The idea is that we're not accepting any kind of sponsorship. We're really looking around for a sponsor that fits, rather than taking the first one that comes along and says, "We'll offer you a lot of money." On this tour we're offering a platform for these people in England called The Friends of the Earth, which is an environmental group, in an effort to really make this tour mean something. Once we've been around this world, I'd like to get back and be able to say that we've said a few important things, rather than drink this product. It's not that we're against sponsors, I just want to find somebody who fits; somebody who we're kind of proud to be associated with, rather than sheer commercialization.

Q: *Your collaboration with Elvis Costello has garnered a lot of attention, and I was wondering if there was anyone in particular that you would love to write with when you start working on your next project.*

A: I don't really have any thoughts about who I might write with next, but I did enjoy writing with Elvis. We wrote nine songs together, four of which have made the albums. There are still five left to do. As far as writing with somebody else, I never really think of those things up front, they just

kind of happen. You run into someone and he says, "Let's write a song, " or I say, "Let's write a song." It's never planned. [Elvis] is a bit of a Beatles fan, and I suspect he's a John fan, you know, 'cause often guys with glasses kind of identified with John. Well, I mean that's true, but he's similar to John in a number of ways, and it wasn't a deterrent. It was good to work with him, mainly just 'cause he's a good writer and he's got a very strong opinion. That's the main thing.

Q: *Have any of your songs been particularly difficult to write?*

A: If you're lucky, songs are easy to come up with; the magic just happens quickly. Some of them you just have to slug at, but the ones I feel lucky are songs like that. "Put It There" was written almost instantly, in two days actually while I was on holiday. Something like "Yesterday," really came without me knowing it. I just woke up one morning.

Q: *Considering that your last few albums have not been blockbusters in the United States, do you have a lot riding on this tour? Do you feel that you have to sort of re-establish yourself with the market?*

A: That's not my prime reason for going out on tour. If you think about it, the first time we ever went out as the Beatles was risky. We were no one, and had to build the whole thing up. I just do my best, go out and try to play some good music and if people come and see me, great. If they buy the album, better.

Q: *Many people have speculated that the success of The Who and Ringo's first tour ever, was what prompted you to go on tour.*

A: I'll tell you who prompted me, and I think them too: The Grateful Dead. If Jerry [Garcia] can still do it that good, there's hope for us all.

Q: *How did Friends of the Earth first come to your attention, and did you start thinking of the environment because of your children or was it be-*

McCartney: 20 Years on His Own

fore then?

A: I think I'm the same as most people in this room and most of the viewers, when this year and last year I was really shocked by the whole environment issue. Once we started to find a hole in the ozone, everyone went, "Uh, oh, someday what's that do to that...?" It questions everything. We've had acid rain for quite a while, we've been dumping nuclear waste and all hell is breaking loose...so I think this year is just one of those years where everyone wants the planet to live on; to be a cool place to live and we do have the power to do that. So that's what you want to be doing, rather than just going around the world, singing songs and making money. Linda and I thought it would be really nice having it mean something by the end of it all. So, yeah, for my kids I'd like the beaches to be able to be played on, to not have pollution. For the sake of the planet, for me, everyone in this room and all the viewers, someone's got to do something. I'm not going to do it single-handed; it's the people who are going to do it, but I have a platform where if I talk about it, maybe people will think about it.

Q: Will you be going to Japan this time?
A: Yes, it's all cleared up.

Q: Why aren't you doing more cities on this tour? It would seem that a lot of people in the middle of the country are going to feel left out.
A: That's always the problem. When we were organizing the tour, we decided to do it two waves when coming to America. The first one is Los Angeles, New York, Chicago and Toronto, and we're doing like four shows in each place. So we're playing to quite a lot of people, but, as you say, it's limited cities. We're hoping to come back

and play more comprehensive dates, where we cover the cities we missed. Because I hate to do that, just come and play the big places. We are coming back, but we haven't got the specific dates yet.

Q: I realize that perhaps there's no other way to do this, but I'm just wondering if you could comment on venues this size and the fact that so many peo-

ple walk away from these concerts thinking they got ripped off, because the sound was bad [NOTE: The Skydome holds just under 60,000 people].

I can't really tell you about that one 'till tonight. I know I don't like going to shows in this size of hall normally, so we'll have to see how we do on this. I haven't done one of these in quite a while. The last thing I did was Seattle Kingdom, which went down very well. Nobody, I don't think, complained. I've got a suspicion nobody's going to complain after tonight, but I'm not going to count my chickens. I saw Genesis at Wembley, the football stadium in England, and I couldn't tell whether Phil Collins was on the stage or not. I think that's a problem, [when] you come out and you're watching tely (television) all evening, when you thought

13

you were going to a concert and you're watching this big screen. I could of stayed at home and done that. I would have been warmer. But we're trying to address those problems. We'll see. We've tried to make the show good wherever we are, even if it's in a pub or a venue this size. The idea is that the music should be good enough to satisfy you, so we'll see how you feel tomorrow. I hope no one feels ripped off.

Q: Why are you coming and playing venues of this size?

A: I'm not having to play venues of this size. The promoter just says, "Would you like to play the Skydome?" and I say, "Yes." Well, you know, I'll play anything. If there's a venue there I normally haven't got anything against them and I'll say the Seattle Kingdom was pretty good.

Q: What made you dedicate "How Many People" off the new album to Chico Mendes?

A: As you said, we dedicated the song which is called "How Many People" to Chico Mendes, whose the guy who got shot trying to save the rain forests. He was a father with a couple of kids, and to me, it just seemed that he didn't need to go out and put his neck on the line to save the forests. Anyone else could have done it, but he went out and did it. I respected that and wanted to dedicate the piece to him because of that, just so people will remember his name, hopefully, in some way. I think the difficult thing about it is that people can't just preach at the Brazilians and say, "Now come on guys, you stop cutting down those forests. We don't cut ours down (wink, wink), so don't you cut yours down." I think we've got to do more than that. I think that governments ought to look at subsidizing people...that means that nations like ours have got to work things out economically so that they can kind of go ahead with what they want to do, but probably stuff that's more expensive so people would have to juggle economics, which is not up to me to do. I'm not really here to preach, it's just that if

someone is going to ask me about it, of course I'm going to respond.

Q: I hear "Motor of Love" from the new album as a religious hymn. Were you trying to lend yourself to a different audience?

A: No, I have this thing that I do which is kind of quasi-religious. I did it in "Let It Be" where I talk about Mother Mary. In fact, the Mother Mary I'm talking about is my own mother, and that song happened because in the Sixties, one night I was a bit sort of freaked out—which happened often in the Sixties, those crazy days, he said, admitting everything—but I was a bit sort of freaked out and I was having a dream and my mother came to me. She died when I was fourteen. She came to me in this dress and said it was alright and it really did make me feel a lot better when I woke up. So I wrote the song, "In my darkest hour Mother Mary comes to me." So So that was that one and that got interesting as being a bit religious. You can take it that way if you want. It works both ways. And in this song "Motor of Love", that you're talking about, I talk about Heavenly Father. I'm actually talking about my dad. "Heavenly Father look down from above." My dad, who hopefully went on top when he died in '76. When I do that, the word Father, generally, in my mind, I'm talking about my father, but I recognize the ambiguity.

Q: Have you and the other Beatles come any closer to settling your business differences?

A: I think we settled. Everything's ready to be signed and we've finally, after 20 years, sorted it all out. We're hoping to sign that very soon.

Q: Any chance of changing George's mind and having him work with you and Ringo?

A: Well, I don't know. George has sort of said there will not be a Beatles reunion. I mean, as far as we're concerned, there can't be a Beatles reunion, because John died and that was the Beatles. I don't think any of us would be interested in substituting someone for John, even Julian, which has been suggested. It wouldn't be the Beatles, it would be a group, so there can't be a Beatles reunion. That's probably what George is talking about. I've only heard this second-hand through these press conferences, but there is a film that we might get around to in a couple of years that we've been meaning to do, and there might possibly be some involvement there where we play together—me, George and Ringo. Now we wouldn't call it a Beatles reunion, but *you* probably would.

Q: We've heard that you're giving away a program book free to all ticketbuyers. I was wondering if you could elaborate on that, what the book is about, why it's free and will there be mass merchandising on your tour?

A: We'll do merchandising, because you know there will be people at the gate with cheap, shoddy stuff, so you've kind of got to do it. The book that we're giving away is just an idea that was cooked up by my manager, actually, while we were planning the tour. You're going to have on your seat a free kind of groovy program, and in it we sort of talk about the band and stuff. We're going to see if it works as an idea. I think it's kind of a nice idea myself.

Q: Any chance that you'll be releasing your Russian album here, or a collection of your oddities and rarities?

A: People have been asking me about the Russian album, but it's just available on import, which is a strange idea—the Russians selling the Americans anything. Originally it was done as sort of a friendship gesture, because Mr. Reagan and Gorbochev were sort of getting it on with Glasnost, and I wanted to be a part of it. That's why it was done, but as to whether or not it will be released here, you have to ask Capital. I think if enough people want it released, it will be.

Q: Have you seen any concerts lately that you've picked something up from that you might be using?

A: I don't normally do that. You don't go to a concert to nick ideas. In fact, you do the opposite. You go to a concert to say, "Okay, we *won't* do that."

Q: Are you planning on an opening act, and if so, who do you have in mind.

A: Actually we decided against an opening act. We were thinking of getting a young band in each town to give them a little bit of exposure, but in fact what I think we're going to do is show a movie up front, which is being worked on at the moment by Richard Lester, the guy who directed **A Hard Day's Night** and **Help**. He's making a movie that shows my historical perspective and then we come on after that. The movie turns into us.

Q: It's been stated that Friends of the Earth will have a platform on this tour, but will any proceeds go to them as well?

A: We haven't thought of that yet, but that's always possible. I don't like to say up front what money's going to go anywhere, but it's quite possible.

Q: You were talking about songs that you never performed live before, and I was wondering if "Hey Jude" is one of them.

A: We are going to do that .

Q: A lot of the bootleg material that has come out has been of very good quality, and I was wondering who controls the rights and will that stuff ever come out?

A: As the Beatles we always looked at artists like Buddy Holly, who, after they died a lot of stuff came out that was a track he'd done on his own, and they got a group together to make it a Buddy Holly record, but we never really liked that. So we were very tidy with most of our material, we erased or got rid of it, so there isn't that much in the way of out-takes. There were two that are quite good. John singing "Leave My Kitten Alone" is quite great, and there are some early things that I think one of these days will be released. There's not much of it, but you probably could make a rarities album.

Q: On tour, Pete Townsend has said that he's not playing as much lead, he's not jumping as much and he's citing his age. Do you see many changes from the way you used to do it?

A: I don't really think so. I've only got one way to do it, and I never figured out how to do it in the first place,

so that's still how I do it. I never jumped as high as Townsend anyway. I just do what I do and I feel very good with this band, which is half the battle really, if you're not worried about them. I don't think you'll see any changes. There aren't many changes in the keys, although I nearly did when I played Prince's Trust on "Long Tall Sally." I was going to take it down from "G" to "E", which is quite a long way down, and I turned up at the show and they said, "Long Tall Sally," and I

said, "Yeah, it's in 'G'." I didn't have the heart to tell them I was taking it down to "E."

Q: I heard that one of the concerts was going to be taped for a Showtime television special. Any comment on that?

A: They're getting a show soon on Showtime that we've already done, so I think that may be the confusion. I don't think there are any plans to tape the concerts as yet. There is a show coming up called "Put It There," which we recorded in England.

Q: You published a book of drawings, and I was wondering if that's something you're still pursuing.

A: That's something I've done since I was a kid, and I enjoy it. I like to paint now, but I really don't have any plans to exhibit it. It's really just for me.

Q: How would you say your audience has changed over the last several years, and do you find yourself writing songs for your listeners, or for yourself?

A: I went through a period of writing for listeners, but I think that's a mistake because you don't really know who's listening anyway, and you tend to sort of write for critics. That's a bad idea, so you have to write for yourself, and that's definitely the way I'm writing now. I figure if I like it, there's a chance that they might. I make a point these days of satisfying meself first.

Q: How much influence has your family life had on your musical career?

A: Consciously I don't sit down and think of family, but obviously as your life changes and you've got four kids like I've got...something like "Put It There" is an expression that my dad used to say to me when I was a kid, and I say it to my kid. So I suppose that's the kind of influence....

Q: About a year ago you were talking about touring in Russia. Is there any chance of that happening?

A: I'd like to go to Russia, particularly now that we've released the album over there and it did well. We looked into doing dates there, but it's the weather. It really is. Napoleon and Hitler ran into the same problem. We opted for Italy instead, but one of these days we'll get there. They may have a warm spell.

Q: The Who has gone Pay-Per-View....

A: I'm not thinking of that at all. At the moment we don't have any plans for it.

Q: Any plans of putting together an autobiography?

A: A couple of years ago I definitely had no plans, because I thought you had to be about 64 at least to write an autobiography. But what's happening for me is that at Ringo's wedding Neil Aspinall, one of the guys who used to work for us at Apple, and I were talking about something, we both had this memory and the only thing that had changed was the backdrop. He remembered the whole incident happening in Picadilly, and I remember the whole incident happening in Saville Row. It was very strange to remember the exact same thing, but the backdrop had changed, but it was something like thirty years ago. So I've actually started to think of maybe writing stuff down,

just to kind of remind myself. I've written a few bits and pieces. I wrote about 20,000 words on the Japanese incident, just really to remind myself what I went through, because I knew I'd forget. I mean I couldn't tell you anything right now. I'd have to read the book meself. So for that kind of reason, just to get the story down as I see it, I'm starting to consider that. There's also a few dodgy books out the last few years that are not based on fact at all. I've got a friend of mine from the Sixties who recently approached me. He wants to do a book. He just did a book on Alan Ginsberg, and it would concentrate on the art rather than which toothpaste I use.

Q: Is there a possibility of getting a live album out of this tour?

A: Yeah, I think so. It depends if we play good. We're definitely thinking about it.

Q: Two quick questions. One, will we ever see a video compilation, because you've done so many of them; and, second, whatever happened to your collaboration with Eric Stewart from Press to Play?

A: The video compilation, yeah, one of these days, probably. No plans at the moment. with Eric. We just made an album together and now he's making his own album. I enjoyed writing with him, he's still a good friend and we could write together in the future. I ended up writing with Elvis for this album, and we enjoyed it, so it's the kind of thing where you choose when the moment comes.

Q: What are your feelings about getting older and still being a rock and roller?

A: Well, you know, I quite like it. Obviously you don't like actually getting older, but I think a lot of people have been encouraged by people like the Grateful Dead. I think there was a time when you thought music equals youth. I don't think it applies anymore. Guys like me or the Rolling Stones will [be going on], and I love the fact that people haven't seen us before. I think it's great, because I've had a lot of nephews or young nieces who kind of say, "Please play it, because we weren't there the first time around." I really like that idea, and I think a lot of the Sixties stuff is coming back, so this is a good time to do it.

Q: Is touring in the 1990s going to be different from touring in the 1960s and 1970s?

A: Yes, it is. Definitely. I have no trepidation at all. The differences will be the technology is better, the sound is better. For me it doesn't really make much difference. It's not to do with the era, it's to do with how good you feel.

Q: It's been a while since you've been on the road. What have been the high points so far and the low points?

A: The high spots so far have been places like Paris, Madrid, Rome and America, really. The other places have all been good—the audiences have all been kind of consistently good—but in places like Rome they're just mad. They're just crazy. It's a party. I think it's the Latin blood. They're just crazy people. Those are probably the high spots. The pitfalls haven't been too many yet. The lights went out in Leone; they were fused a bit. Otherwise just trying to make sure I don't lose me voice is the only other thing. I'm singing about two hours a night, which is way too much for anyone.

Q: What's different about your current band and Wings?

A: I don't know really. We're doing a couple of things different. They're good musicians, which doesn't mean that the other people weren't, but they are all good players, so when we jam we tend to make sort of a halfway decent noise, instead of kind of out of tune and stuff. Certainly the Beatles were good at that. I think the main difference from Wings, particularly, is that actually they're very easygoing kind of people. We're all older and wiser now, so we don't party all night, just so we can come here, talk to you and look halfway alive in the morning. A couple of the guys have kids, families

and stuff, so it's a little bit more of a regular crowd than with Wings, which was a bit more of a partying group. Which is great, if you can take the pace.

Q: What did you think of your first New York performance?

A: Good. We had to work a little harder last night. Some of the gigs we've been going to, you really haven't even had to work. It was more like going to a party, they were in such a ridiculous mood. Like Chicago was very silly. I think it was a little bit of a charity audience in here as well last night. There were a few people in pinstriped shirts looking at you like, "Entertain me," which is okay. You've got to work a little harder, that's all.

Q: You are the first of the Beatles to be going to Brazil, and you're arriving there at a moment when Brazilians are very sensitive about the media and people around the world who mention their role in the destruction of the rain forests. As you're going there as a Friend of the Earth, what's the message you're bringing to Brazilians?

A: I understand their sensitivity. It's a very tough thing the rest of the world saying to them, "You can't make money cutting down your rain forest, but we can." I sympathize with that. It's a difficult issue really. The whole thing about Friends of the Earth, as I've said, is that it's very nearly boring. People kind of yawn and say, "Great, let somebody else sort it out." But we've got to address it and they've got to be included. I don't really know how you do it, but I think they've got to help in sorting it out. I don't think it's good enough for people to point their hand at Brazil and say, "Hey, you're spoiling our planet." England is certainly very guilty of exporting things like acid rain. I think we've all got to get together and sort it out, instead of blaming one country.

Q: How did it feel to play the Beatles songs last night?

A: It really feels good playing those songs, and there are two reasons for that. One, we never really did them much with the Beatles. "Get Back" we just did in **Let It Be.** We made it up during that film and played it on the roof, and I never really played it again. So it was really nice to get back to those songs, because they're fresh. For me, anyway. I've been doing all the other material a lot more often. So it feels really good to do, and I think the audience likes them. You see people in the audience kind of my age with kids and stuff, and you see grown men crying. There's a lot of emotion involved, because I think it reminds people of either a better time or when they were first courting. These songs tend to take people back, which is obvious, but you take 'em back to a good place, which isn't so obvious. It's really good being the person singing the song when you see them going through all that stuff.

Q: Is it tough remembering all the lyrics?
A: In a way for me it's a bit like a stage play. I've got to remember this play with all these words. As I say, these are songs I haven't done for a while. I probably get about two or three lines wrong each night, but I call it different arrangements. I'll bluff my way out of anything.

Q: What goes through your mind when you come back to New York?
A: It's always good memories for me. Plus my wife was born here. It's a great place. It's the city to be in. I met Ed Sullivan on the street once. He didn't recognize me. I said, "Hey, Ed, I was on your show, man." [Does Beatles woooooo sound] And he said, "Oh, yeah. Sure."

Q: What influence has classical music had on your music?
A: When I was a kid, I never really listened to any classical music at all. My dad was kind of a jazzer, so he used to turn it off if it ever came on the radio. When I got older and kind of started writing music and went into sessions where strings were used and hearing the orchestra warming up, I really got into it. It was George Martin's sugges-tion to do string quartet on "Yesterday." I said, "String quartet on a Beatles song?" He said, "Trust me. Let's just try it." So I sat down with him, arranged it, put a couple of odd-ball things in just to put my identity on it, and I was very pleased with the way it turned out. Then we went on to do "Eleanor Rigby," "She's Leaving Home," John did "Walrus." So we messed around quite a bit with it. Now it's culminated with me actually being asked to do a piece for 1991 with a New York guy who works in England called Carl Davis, who's a conductor. It's for the Liverpool Cathedral and the Liverpool Philharmonic Orchestra, so we're actually writing it. That's a full blown classical piece and we're up to the fourth movement, which is really exciting for me. It's a real stretch. Something I've never done, and it's working out quite well.

Q: It's been announced that VISA will be underwriting your tour. Do you think you're selling out?
A: I don't feel I have to apologize. It seems to me that we're in a fairly obvious capitalist society. We all accept money for what we do. You all expect money from what you do. If you go in to your boss you want to get the best deal you can get. You don't say, "Give me the lowest wage you can think of, boss." I'm the same. We've never been any different. Somebody said the other day that the Beatles were anti-materialism. No they weren't. We may have suggested in our theories that it wasn't the greatest thing—I still don't think it's the greatest thing—but I have no problem accepting money. The only thing is if I have to hold up a bottle of something. That's what I've resisted all my career. I think sometimes you can over-commercialize a thing, but the way we've tried to do this thing with VISA...it was put to me the way they did the Olympics. You never got the feeling that the Olympics was promoting the card. It was the other way around, and I'm hoping that's the way it's going to look with what they're going to be doing for us. It's really just a business deal, and I'm in business.

The point is, in the economics of a tour like this, just getting from place to place is a big expense, and so these days most people accept some kind of sponsorship, so we held out for one of the obvious ones and we've gone with this one, which—I think—once you see the actual commercials, you'll agree there is no real sell-out.

Q: Do you still feel strong against using your music in other commercials for other products?

A: Yeah, I mean I see a difference here. I wish I had the commercial to show you and I haven't even seen it. I think there is a difference using songs like "All You Need is Love" to kind of promote a product and, you know, using them sort of like in a movie or something. I think actually once they get identified with a specific product, like all the things that people have been doing for soft drinks, there is a difference and that kind of commercial I wouldn't do.

I have been offered a lot of money to hold up a whiskey bottle in Japan, which I don't want to do, though, 'cause that is what I call a commercial. I think if these people you are talking about, VISA, want to film us, film this, show the tour, show moments from the show, show me getting in and out of limos and then talk about their card without me ever actually turning to the viewer and saying, "Yes, this card...," [I have no problem with it]. In fact, we are kind of irreligious about it, we do sound checks where we advertise all the other cards.

Q: Do you read your own reviews?

A: No I don't, actually. I hear I've been getting some real good ones. To me, it's like watching rushes. It puts me off. All I've got to do is see one sentence.. To tell you truth, I did read one. Somebody said, "You've got the greatest review in LA," and I said, "I don't like to do this, but if it's the greatest, I'm going to read it." I read it, it was gush, gush, brilliant brilliant, and then he said, "The low point of the show was 'Ebony and Ivory.'" Every night since then I've tried working the death

out of that song. It's just one guy's opinion. Some people pick on it, but what else is new.

Q: I understand the Beatles met Elvis. What was that like?

A: It was a great evening. I've heard since that people said it was weird, he was all drugged out, we were crazy...it wasn't. It was a very straight evening. We were major fans of Elvis, particularly his work before he joined the army. Just to set the record straight, it was a great evening. He was really brilliant. He was the first guy I'd ever seen who had a remote control on his television—that's how long ago it was—Priscilla was kind of wheeled in for about ten minutes, kind of like she was a doll and she looked like one, but it was great. We were totally in awe of him. He was learning to play bass, so I kind of taught him a little bit of stuff. A really nice guy, regular person.

Q: Considering all the problems you've had with the law, do you favor the legalization of marijuana?

A: I favor the decriminalization of it, because I think you've got too many people who get into it innocently who become criminals. The minute you're caught and the minute you go into the slammer, you learn worse tricks. I think it's a very difficult issue. I don't want to defend it too much, because if my kids ask me, I say, "Don't do any kind of drugs, stay clean. That's definitely the best way to be in life." The argument comes up when people say, "Scotch is legal and pot isn't." At that point I think there probably is a good argument for decriminalization.

Q: Let's talk about recording studios themselves. Could you tell me how you view recording back in the Beatles days to now? I mean, is it more fun? You've spent thirty years in the studio.

A: Well, the main difference is it used to be a lot quicker to record, you know. We recorded the first Beatles album in a day from ten in the morning to ten at night. We did "Twist and

Shout" last, because if we'd done it first, we couldn't have done any of the others, you know. John's voice would have gone. So one day for an album was pretty fast. Now it takes one day to switch on the machines, load the computer, find out where the on/off switch is. That's the main difference. It just takes forever now to record one song, whereas you used to do a whole album in a day. But the nearest I got to it recently was doing that Russian album. I did [lots] of rock and roll songs. We did eighteen songs in a day and it was really good. I think it's more fun to record that way, very spontaneous and immediate. The other is like—God, honest it's terrible—you get this computer-down time. The other great fun thing you get—and you probably all get it too—it takes like five hours for the guys to fix the computer, which was introduced to make things cheaper and quicker.

Q: Is there a great deal of unreleased material by the Beatles?
A: The best thing in the archives that's unreleased is "Leave My Kitten Alone," which is an oldie. I think that's quite a good track that's worthy of release. And me, John and George singing harmony on "Three Cool Cats" is quite nice. I think a lot of the rest of it are just alternate tapes that we kind of turned down, and they're bringing 'em back now, calling them "real interesting takes." They're actually the takes we rejected, but they can probably get another **Gone With the Wind** out of the out-takes.

Q: How do you see life in the Nineties?
The Nineties is going to be the time when people finally realize we've got to clean this world up, and it's going to be the time when we do it in order to have a clean 21st Century. That's my wish, anyway. Optimistic?

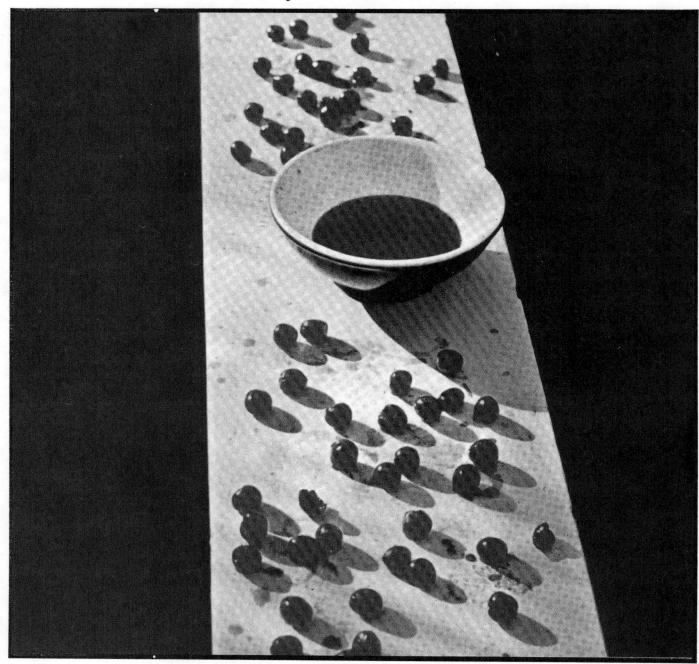

McCartney Album Tracks: "The Lovely Linda," "That Would Be Something," "Valentine Day," "Every Night," "Hot As Sun Glasses," "Junk," "Man We Was Lonely," "Oo You," "Momma Miss America," "Teddy Boy," "Singalong Junk," "Maybe I'm Amazed," "Kreen—Akrore"

McCartney sold over three million copies, spending three weeks at number one on the American charts and number two for the same amount of time on the British charts

II. McCARTNEY

Q:
Is your break
with the Beatles tem-
porary or permanent, due to
personal differences or musical ones?

A:

Personal differences, business differences, but most of all, because
I have a better time with my family. Temporary or permanent? I don't know.

Q: Do you foresee a time when Lennon/McCartney becomes an active songwriting
partnership again?

A: No.

> *——Taken from a press release from Paul McCartney announcing his split from*
> *the Beatles in April, 1970*

As the 1960s came to an end, so did the Beatles. They epitomized the preceding ten years, launching or standing in the forefront of a cultural revolution that altered the face of America and most of the free world.

For this precise reason Paul McCartney felt trepidation about his future as a solo artist. Although publicly he put on as brave a face as possible, privately he was uneasy. Battling his former mates and the breakup itself only complicated matters.

From a historical perspective, **McCartney** is interesting. That entire album was done by Paul himself, with Paul writing all the songs and Paul playing all the instruments. The record has a rough edge to it, which, over the years, has added to its charm.

"The **McCartney** album was good fun, because I got a machine from EMI, only a four track, and I just had it in my living room," McCartney's explained. "It was a very *free* album for me to do, because I'd get up and think about breakfast and then wander into the living room to do a track. It's got that feel and there's a lot of stuff that you, the listener, might have thought twice about, but I didn't. It was very interesting to do and it had a certain kind of rawness.

"I rather fancied having just the plain tapes and nothing done to them at all. [The Beatles] had thought of doing something looser before, but the albums always turned out to be well-produced. So when **McCartney** came along, I had all these rough things and I liked them all and thought, 'Well, they're rough, but they've got that certain kind of thing about them, so we'll leave it and just put it out.' It's not an album which was really sweated over, and yet now I find it's a lot of people's favorites. They think it's great to hear the kids screaming and the door opening.

"In the back of everyone's mind, there was always that kind of thing. The sound of a tape being spooled back is an interesting sound. If you're working in a recording studio, you hear it all the time and get used to it. You don't think anything of it. But when the man switches on the tape machine in the middle of the track and you hear that kind of 'djeeow' and the track starts. I'd always liked all that, all those rough edges and loose ends. It gives a kind of live excitement. I like to surprise myself. I like to catch myself out, because it's too easy to be predictable. So there are a few little things on there. Probably the best songs were 'Maybe I'm Amazed' and 'Every Night.' I like some of the other stuff—slightly experimental stuff—just because I was allowing myself to be experimental."

The experimental nature of **McCartney**, coupled with the then recent Beatles breakup with McCartney seen as the one responsible, led to merciless attacks on the album. Actually, it's not a bad collection. Yet it's something of a letdown compared to the Beatles.

Pleasant surprises include "That Would Be Something," "Every Night" (a live and somewhat superior version of which can be found on the **Concerts for the People of Kampuchea** album), "Man We Was Lonely" and "Teddy Boy."

"They were almost throwaways, you know," McCartney has commented. "But that's why they were included, they weren't *quite* throwaways. Like 'Momma Miss America.' I like them when I hear them now, thinking, 'Did I do that? Boy, that was cheeky!' Generally you wouldn't do an instrumental; McCartney things tend to always have a vocal."

"Teddy Boy" is interesting in that the track had originally been included in the George Martin produced version of the **Get Back** album, before Phil Spector took over the project and its title was changed to **Let It Be.**

"It was from the Beatles period," McCartney concurred. "There was always a song that'd lie around for a couple of years, with one good part and you'd mean to finish it one day. The words 'teddy boy' to English people had always meant what you might have called a 'hood' in America. To us, it was these fellas in Edwardian long coats, a big fashion when I was growing up. I also have a cousin Ted, so he was the other meaning."

The standout cut is "Maybe I'm Amazed," a McCartney classic that ranks among his best work.

"That was very much a song of the period," he pointed out. "When you're in love with someone—I mean, God, this

sounds soppy—but when you are in love and it's a *new* love like that, as it was for me and Linda with the Beatles breaking up, that was my feeling. Maybe I'm amazed at what's going on—maybe I'm not—but *maybe I am!* 'Maybe I'm amazed at the way you pulled me out of time, hung me on the line.' There were things happening at the time and these phrases were my symbols for them. And other people seemed to understand. At the time we thought [it] was a good track and maybe we should do that as a single, which it probably should have been. But we never did."

Instead he issued a single featuring "Another Day," backed with "Oh Woman, Oh Why" (which reached number three in America and number one in Britain, and which, can respectively be found on the **Wings Greatest** and **Wild Life** CDs).

Regarding the writing of "Another Day," McCartney told one journalist, "Anyone who was around back then was bored with stories of the Beatles breakup, the business disputes and all these negative things that were going on. It wasn't really difficult to know what to do, 'cause you were either going to say, 'Okay, I've been a Beatle and now I'll go back to the sweet shop or do something else with my life.' Or, 'I'll try to continue in music!' But then the thought came, 'Yeah, but you're gonna have to try and *top* the Beatles' and that's not an easy act to follow. It was intimidating to even *think* of staying in the music business. If we'd gotten too paranoid about it, we *wouldn't* have. So we ended up in New York, and 'Another Day' was one of the first tracks released with that attitude. I'd been working with Phil Ramone at his studio doing tracks for **Ram**. We were hanging out and having a great time, and one of the songs that we had that sounded good was 'Another Day.' We did a mix on it, and it was the first one that I thought, 'That would make a good choice for a single.' It was as simple as that."

"Another Day" can be viewed as the flip-side of "Yesterday." Yearning for the past transforms into acceptance of the present and moving ahead with the daily motions in life, no matter how mundane they may seem. The song seemed symbolic of the public's perception of a McCartney searching for musical direction.

Despite positive sales response, McCartney was stunned by the critical trashing. It intensified his disorientation after the break-up.

Even former-partner John Lennon got into the act. He declared **McCartney** "rubbish. I think he'll make a better one, when he's frightened into it. I expected just a little more."

Insecurities weren't lessened when, a month later, McCartney found himself in competition with the album and film **Let It Be**, a considerable let-down from its Beatles predecessor, **Abbey Road**, despite having been recorded earlier. Ironically, the film and album serve as two opposing views of the group's demise. The former stands as visual testament to these four guys simply not enjoying each other's company anymore. They were all suffocating from close and restricting artistic proximity. The latter, despite misdirected production by Phil Spector, offers a much more positive image, harkening back to the original **Get Back** premise showing the band returning to their roots and a time when the music was pure without studio over-dubbing. It concluded with the same line John Lennon had uttered at the film's conclusion, "Thank you, folks, and on behalf of the group and myself, I hope we passed the audition."

The circle was complete. As the "audition" that started it all came to a close, the four individuals within that circle were out on their own. And throughout 1970, when McCartney came up against the other three in the marketplace, reviews would *not* always be in his favor.

Ringo's **Beaucops of Blues**, a collection of country oldies, did not fare very well. But George Harrison, who had come into his own with the "Something" and "Here Comes the Sun"

compositions on **Abbey Road**, proved he was full of surprises. He had developed a backlog of material waiting for the opportunity to include them on Beatles albums. The result was **All Things Must Pass**, which scored big. It's most significant to compare the **McCartney** album to John Lennon's **Plastic Ono Band**. The listener sees how the former songwriting partners approach their craft.

Everyone knew Lennon and McCartney were moving in separate musical directions, a point emphasized by the two releases. McCartney, often accused of being too sweet and sentimental, and Lennon, with biting lyrics, had always kept each other in check. Now they were on their own. And it was reflected in the music, each going a bit overboard. **Plastic Ono Band** was Lennon's so-called "Primal Scream," for the most part brilliant, but the unadulterated pain unleashed is startling. The **McCartney** album, for all its virtues, pales by lyrical comparison. There is no doubt *everyone* was making that comparison.

That year Lennon noted prophetically that **Plastic Ono Band** would probably "scare [Paul] into doing something decent, and then he'll scare me into doing something decent. I think he's capable of great work, and I think he will do it. I wish he wouldn't, you know. I wish nobody would. In me heart of hearts, I wish I was the only one in the world or whatever it is. But I *can't* see Paul doing it twice."

Lennon was right. But the journey would not be an easy one.

Ram Album Tracks: "Too Many People," "3 Legs," "Ram On," "Dear Boy," "Uncle Albert/Admiral Halsey," "Smile Away," "Heart of the Country," "Monkberry Moon Delight," "Eat at Home," "Long Haired Lady," "Ram On," "The Back Seat of My Car"

RAM sold over a million copies in America alone, where it spent two weeks at number two, and three weeks at the same spot on the British charts.

III. RAM

After the critical assault, McCartney realized he would have to get down and dirty. He could then rise to the challenge of his solo career. To this end, he and wife Linda went to New York and began auditioning musicians for the next album, **Ram**. Denny Seiwell was taken on as drummer, with Dave Spinoza and Hugh McCracken as guitarists. In addition, McCartney involved the New York Philharmonic Orchestra on three tracks, "Uncle Albert/Admiral Halsey," "Long Haired Lady" and "The Back Seat of My Car."

"Linda and I mainly [did] all the harmonies," McCartney's explained. "God...I worked her on that album. Because she hadn't done an awful lot, so it was a little bit out of tune. She understood that it had to be good and you couldn't let any shit through. I gave her a hard time, I must say, but we were pleased with the results. It paid off for us. It was very much us against the world at that point."

McCartney has noted, "(The title) **Ram** seemed like a good word because it not only meant ram forward, press on, be positive and those kinds of things, but I also was letting a lot of people know...we're into sheep, actually, and have been for a number of years. When I bought my Scottish farm, I inherited a flock. Just keeping them alive over the years, I got interested, and ram is a male sheep. Beyond that, I don't really know. We had a photo of me with a ram and we did our own art work. It was kind of a funky period for Linda and I in those early days. Both of us had gotten into the artsy thing, me with the Beatles and she with photography. We were well slated."

Ram, like **McCartney**, was ravaged by the critics. Perhaps unfairly so. Far from a classic, it falls between its ragged-edged predecessor and a polished studio album. **Ram** features strong compositions, including "Too Many People," "Dear Boy," "The Back Seat of My Car" and "Uncle Albert/Admiral Halsey".

"Too Many People" is McCartney speaking out against those who preach, while "Dear Boy" allows him to reflect on "someone" he feels should regret no longer being together, because he's doing just fine, thank you very much. It may ring false, but it seemed an appropriate shield to block detractors.

"The Back Seat of My Car" is an enjoyable, though harmless, semi-rocker, while "Uncle Albert/Admiral Halsey" offers an infectious tune that plays as if he had composed it during his Beatles days. Like many of those songs (i.e. "We Can Work It Out," "A Day in the Life"), it seems like two sets of lyrics grafted together. In Britain, "The Back Seat of My Car" was released as a single backed with "Heart of the Country," and only reached number 39; in America, "Uncle Albert" was issued, backed with "Too Many People," and eventually climbed to number one. It was his first solo single to do so.

McCartney has explained, "I had an Uncle Albert; I was sort of thinking of him. He was an uncle who died when I was a kid, a good bloke who used to get drunk and stand on the table and read passages from *The Bible*, at which point people used to laugh. A lot. But he's someone I recalled fondly, and when the song was coming it was like a nostalgic thing. 'I think I'm gonna rain' was the wistful line, really, and I thought of him. I never can explain why I think of a particular person

public feud that would continue for years to come. Lennon's next album, **Imagine**, contained "How Do You Sleep?," an unbridled attack on McCartney.

"It was like Dylan doing 'Like a Rolling Stone,' one of his nasty songs," Lennon said. "It's using somebody as an object to create something. I wasn't really feeling that vicious at the time, but I *was* using my resentment towards Paul to create a song. Let's put it that way. It was just a mood. Paul took it the way he did because it obviously, pointedly, refers to him, and people just hounded him about it, asking, 'How do ya feel about it?' But there were a few little digs on *his* albums, which he kept so obscure that other people didn't notice 'em, you know. But *I* heard them. So I just thought, well, hang up being obscure! I'll just get right down to the nitty-gritty."

While Lennon plays down the intensity of his attack, McCartney says the entire situation was blown out of proportion. "Okay, there was a little bit of it from my point of view," he's said, "certain little lines, I'd be thinking, 'Well, this will get him.' You do, you know. Christ, you can't avoid it. 'Too Many People' I wrote a little bit in that, 'too many people preaching.' That was actually the only thing I was saying referring to John at the time."

While McCartney may consider this true, there are things on **Ram** that belie this proclamation of innocence, besides"Too Many People." For instance, "Dear Boy" can also be seen as a subtle statement against Lennon, and the back cover of the album features a photo of a pair of beetles fornicating, which must have conveyed something to an ex-Beatle. Still, it is possible Lennon made too big a deal out of these things. One really does wonder whether they warranted the viciousness of "How Do You Sleep?"

McCartney still had another debacle awaiting him in the form of **Wild Life**, before he would get his career back.

when I write. 'We're so sorry, Auntie Edna'—you know, it could have been her. I use these things like a painter uses colors. I don't know where I got Halsey's name, but you read it in magazines and sometimes they just fall into your songs, because they scan so well."

Undoubtedly, McCartney, who had been criticized for self-indulgence on his initial effort, was shocked by the negative critical reaction to **Ram**. He brought more musicians into the studio and delivered what he thought was a more "professional" album.

"There were a lot of bum notices after **Ram**," he's admitted. "But I keep meeting people wherever I go, like I met someone skiing. As he skied past me, he said, 'I loved **Ram**, Paul.' So that's really what I go by, just the kind of people who flash by me in life. Just ordinary people and they say they loved it. That's why I go a lot by sales, not just for the commercial thing. Like if a thing sells well, it means a lot of people bought it and liked it. It's funny, you know. People have these different favorites and sometimes they want to pick the offbeat ones that didn't do well, just to be cool. There's something in all those albums, even if they're my worst ones. I know I did them intending for them to be the greatest things I ever did."

John Lennon viewed subtle portions of **Ram** as a personal attack. It began a

3 BONUS TRACKS

Wings Wild Life

Wild Life Album Tracks: "Mumbo," "Bip Bop," "Love is Strange," "Wild Life," "Some People Never Know," "I Am Your Singer," "Bip Bop Link," "Tomorrow," "Dear Friend," "Mumbo Link," "Oh Woman, Oh Why"*, "Mary Had a Little Lamb"* and "Little Woman Love"*

Wild Life reached number 10 on the American charts, while it peaked at number 11 in Britain.

IV. WILD LIFE

Reeling
from   critical
bombardment, the famous
Lennon interviews in **Rolling Stone**
which dismissed him as another Engelbert
Humperdinck, and the lyrical assault of "How Do You
Sleep?," McCartney reassessed his solo career and concluded
that he needed a band.

"What else do I do?" he'd asked. "Get together a very big famous group? The other guys did that all the time, which is probably why I didn't want to do it. It just felt too safe for me. I just felt, like no, got to risk it a bit more. I had decided early on that I wanted to carry on being a singer and working with a band, but I had no band. I thought, 'Well, if I don't sing for a year, I'm going to get croaky. And if I don't sing for two years, I'm going to think that I'm not a singer anymore.' So I had to try and get a band together, just to give me something to do and keep me off the streets. That's when I started to put Wings together."

McCartney actually considered the monikers Turpentine and The Dazzlers before settling on Wings, a name he came up with while wife Linda was in the hospital giving birth to their second child. "We were in King's College Hospital and our baby was in intensive care, so rather than just sitting around twiddling my thumbs, I was thinking of hopeful names for a new group, and somehow this uplifting idea of Wings came to me exactly at that time. It just sounded right. If it could happen, I'd [have just liked] to call it Wings and everyone knows that that's the band with Paul McCartney in it, but I don't think I could. So basically we just call it Paul McCartney and Wings. Whoever joins is stuck with that. It's a slight hang-up, but it shouldn't really be a big one. Anyone who's interested in music shouldn't be too hung up by the fact that I'm the front man."

The initial Wings line-up consisted of Paul, Linda, drummer Denny Siewell and Denny Laine, former guitarist with the Moody Blues. There was no question that it was McCartney's show. In picking the band members, he's explained: "Danny Siewell had done sessions on **Ram**. He did a good job and we liked each other, so he was in. Denny Laine I knew from the Moody Blues, and I'd always liked his voice and stuff, so I thought he might be a good person to work with. Our voices kind of complemented each other, and we had a few things in common in our background. Linda, really I just wanted my mate from this period on stage with me, so I kind of said to her, 'You've not really played piano or keyboard before, but do you want to try being in the band?' I must admit that we talked about the glamor, like you do when you're starting a thing. You don't talk about the down side, 'Oh my God, there's going to come a time when we're not going to have a hit.' You talk about going on stage, the applause, the lights, so we talked in those kinds of terms and she said, 'Great, it'll be fun.'"

The band immediately went into the studio, inspired by Bob Dylan. They emerged with McCartney's biggest solo fiasco, **Wild Life**.

"I must say," he's admitted, "you have to like me to like the record. I mean, if it's just taken cold...it wasn't that brilliant as a recording. We did it in about two weeks, the whole thing. And it had been done on that kind of a buzz. We'd been hearing about how Dylan had come in and done everything in one take. I think in fact that we never gave the engineer a chance to even set up the balance."

McCartney: 20 Years on His Own

There's no denying **Wild Life** is McCartney's weakest album. A perfectionist like McCartney should *never* rush an album within a two week timeframe. The result is a number half-baked tracks, with others which shouldn't have been included at all—such as two instrumentals.

There are a few tracks worth listening to, most notably, "Love is Strange" (though it loses points because it isn't *his* song), "Some People Never Know," a very pleasant ballad deserving more attention than its garnered, and "Dear Friend," his lyrical attempt at reconciliation with Lennon.

In the past, McCartney's commented on reaction to the album and his aim in writing "Dear Friend." He noted, "It's like when I'm talking to people about Picasso or something, and they say, 'Well, his blue period was the only one that was any good.' But for me, if the guy does some great things then even his down moments are interesting. His lesser moments, rather, because they make up the final picture. Some moments seem less. He was going through kind of a pressure period. You know, you can't live your life without pressure periods. No one I know has.

"['Dear Friend'] was written for John—to John. It was like a letter. With the business pressures of the Beatles breaking up, it's like a marriage. One minute you're in love, the next minute you hate each other's guts. I don't think any of us really ever got to the point where we *actually* hated each other's guts, but the business people involved were pitting us against each other. It's a pity, because it's very difficult to cut through all that, and what can you do? You can't write a letter saying, 'Dear pal of mine, I love you'—it's all a bit too much. So you do what we all seemed to do, which was write it in songs. I wrote 'Dear Friend' as a kind of peace gesture."

As 1972 rolled in, McCartney's self esteem took another hit from George Harrison's **The Concerts For Bangla Desh**, which was greeted by nearly unanimous raves. In fact one has to wonder whether McCartney's ever regretted not participating in the event just to avoid having it perceived as a Beatles reunion.

Guitarist Henry McCullough joined Wings just in time to record "Give Ireland Back to the Irish" (number twenty one in America, thirteen in Britain), written in response to the "Bloody Sunday" massacre. It was his only political song in the Lennon mode.

"Before I did that [song], I always used to think, 'God, John's crackers doing all these political songs,'" he's explained. "I always vowed that I'll be the one who doesn't do political songs. It didn't seem appropriate, but you suddenly realize that you've got people listening to you like [Live Aid's Bob] Geldorf does. He's got a respect in the world beyond his desires, and when you get that big you realize you've got the power to influence people's thinking. So instead of being like Hitler and using the music as a propaganda machine, we've tried to sort of angle it, always, to general issues for humanity. [In this case] what happened over there was they had this massacre when some people had been doing a peaceful demonstration. Paratroopers went in and killed a few people, a bit like Kent State. So we were against the Irish; it was like being at war with them. And I'd grown up with this thing that the Irish are our *brothers*. Suddenly we're killing our buddies, and I thought, 'Wait a minute, this is *not* clever, and I wish to protest on behalf of us people.' So I tried it. It was number one in Ireland and, funnily enough, it was number one in Spain of all places. I don't think Franco could have understood."

The single, which is a bit difficult for an American to get behind, was promptly banned by the BBC. McCartney responded three months later with his version of "Mary Had a Little Lamb," backed with "Little Woman Love" (number twenty eight in America, six in Britain), almost as if to say: "Here, ban this!"

McCartney didn't agree, "I didn't give that much thought to it. I've got a daughter named Mary and she always pricks up her ears at this tune. I

33

thought I'd record a song for her," he said, while admitting, "I do things that aren't necessarily thought out. I had an idea in my head that it would be interesting for everyone to find out what the words to the original nursery rhyme were. I thought it was all very deep and all very nice, and would make a nice little children's song, like 'Yellow Submarine.' I see now, you know, it wasn't much of a record."

Putting censorship of "Give Ireland Back to the Irish" and the mediocrity of "Mary Had a Little Lamb" behind him, McCartney got Wings on the road, though not exactly on a world tour.

"With Wings I didn't feel it was a good idea after the Beatles to come out with a little group that wasn't rehearsed, so we had to find some way of getting to know each other, playing the songs to the audience. When the Beatles had broken up, my feelings of what the group had needed was to go back to grass roots and go and play a few little working man clubs, and perform on small stages. We'd fallen out over this. John hadn't agreed, and that's when he sort of announced his resignation from the group. So I thought that's what I'd do with Wings. Instead of doing what was expected, I asked myself, 'What do I *really* want to do?' What have I missed being with the Beatles? What is it time to do?' I didn't want to go to Carnegie Hall with this ropey band that had never played [live] together, so what we did, we all piled in a van and just took off up the motorway. Finally we wound up at Nottingham University and just went in and said, 'Hello, we're here and would you like us to play?' And they couldn't believe it, you know, they kind of leaped around and stuff and then they said, 'Yeah, of course. Come back tomorrow at lunch time and we'll have it all set up for you.' So I did my first concert since leaving the Beatles at Nottingham University. I think we had ten songs that lasted about three minutes, all of them played very fast and nervously, and then we'd repeat them all and pretend they were requests. For me, this was like going back to the Cavern, a whole new life starting again. After that, we just went

around and when we turned up at a town we'd say, 'Excuse me, have you got a university?,' and if they did, we'd just pull up there.

"With the Beatles, you used to get paid massively, but you never saw it, because it always went straight into the company. You had to draw on it. So for me, one of the big buzzes of that first tour was actually getting a bag of coins at the end of the gig. It wasn't just a materialistic thing—it was the feeling of getting physically paid again; it was like going back to square one. I wanted to take it back to where the Beatles started, which was in the halls. We charged 50 pence to get in—obviously we could have charged more—and gave the Student Union a bit for having us there. We played poker with the money afterwards, and I'd actually pay the band physically, you know, '50 pence for you...and 50 pence for you.' It brought back the thrill of actually working for a living."

The "thrill" lasted two weeks, with stops in Swansea, Birmingham, Salford, Sheffield, Leeds, Newcastle, Scarborough, Hull and York. Wings, particularly McCartney, now had the confidence to take on the world, beginning in Europe with 26 dates in nine countries. McCartney admitted to being nervous at the prospect of touring again, which is why he chose Europe instead of Britain or the United States.

"We wanted to start at quite a smallish place," he commented in regards to their first performance at France's Chateau Vallon in July of 1972. "We're going to appear in England, but if you go and play Britain or America with a very new band, you're really on the spot. You've got to be red hot. It takes a little time for a band to get red hot."

In 1980, he explained how this had applied to the Beatles at the beginning of the Sixties. "We had cooked up this whole new British thing; we had a long time to work it out and make all our mistakes in Hamburg with almost no one watching. One of the big things about the Beatles, which I always think new groups should take as a bit of advice, was that we were cheeky enough to say we won't go to the States until we've got a number one record. It's a pretty cheeky kind of thing. There are a lot of artists still from here (England) who go over and vanish.

"The main thing I didn't want to face was the torment of five rows of press people with little pads all looking and saying, 'Oh well, he's not as good as he was.' So we decided to go out on that university tour, which made me less nervous, because it was less of a big deal. We went out on that tour and by the end of that I felt quite ready for something else and we went to Europe. That was a bit more of a big deal, 'Here he is, ladies and gentlemen, sold all the tickets out.' I had to go on with a band I really didn't know much."

Wings would not perform any Beatles songs; they would rise or fall on solo material. "It was good fun," he's admitted. "It was just the climate that was a problem. We really felt we could never be as good as the Beatles. It's a little bit of a pity, in a way. If we'd never had the Beatles thing, we could have really rejoiced in all the fun and success we were having. [Also], the Beatles things are a bit close for me to do at the moment. Although when we were on holiday recently, I was rediscovering 'Yesterday', playing it on an acoustic guitar. I love 'em, you know. I enjoyed it all. Fantastic thing while it lasted, but for me, I don't like the idea of having been in the World Cup and sitting around living on your laurels, just because you won the World Cup four years ago. I like football, you know the analogy. I like to keep truckin'. I like the idea of being in a working band."

McCartney pointed out that some of his nervousness had dissipated by the close of the European tour. His confidence grew during the ensuing British tour in early 1973, his triumphantly hailed return to the concert world.

"For the first few months," McCartney said, "I thought, 'Oh Christ, it'll never work, they'll criticize us every time we open our mouths, because we're not the Beatles. But it's worked out. We're growing. I'm satisfied with how we are

now. I think I'm good. I like me. I'm good. I can dig me. Can you? I know some night you can't, but I try to understand that side, just as there are some nights I might not dig you even though *you* do."

Between early 1972 and mid 1973, several interesting things happened. In September John Lennon released **Some Time in New York City**, greeted by the kind of reviews that met McCartney's first few efforts. And followed with the single "Happy Xmas"/"Listen, The Snow is Falling," a moderate hit which has become a Christmas standard.

Counterpointing Lennon's decline, McCartney scored with "Hi Hi Hi"/"C Moon" (number 10 in America, number three in Britain), a double-sided single that got feet tapping and indicated that something *very* special was happening to his music. Finally, the critics began to rave over a post-Beatles track penned by him. "Hi Hi Hi" was also banned by the BBC.

"I never set out in any way to be controversial. It just doesn't interest me to be that. Whenever we *did* get banned, we'd get these telegrams, from Yoko Ono mostly, saying, 'Congratulations, you're getting really underground.' The great laugh is when we go live it makes a great announcement. You can say, 'This one was banned,' and everyone goes 'Hooray!' The audience loves it, you know. Everyone's a bit anti-all-that-banning; all that censorship. Our crew, our generation, really doesn't dig that stuff. I think now, [though, the song is] kind of dated, it's got words and phrases in it like 'bootleg' and 'We're gonna get high in the midday sun,' and it's very much a song of the times when there were festivals and everyone had long hair, flared trousers and jackets. Very 60s. To me, that was my parting shot to those days."

Wings played over thirty dates during their tour of Britain, winning over even the most stubborn critics. But, still, there was one thing missing, looming on the horizon across the waters: America!

It was still three years away.

Red Rose Speedway Album Tracks: "Big Barn Bed," "My Love," "Get on the Right Thing," "One More Kiss," "Little Lamb Dragonfly," "Single Pigeon," "When the Night," "Loup (1st Indian on the Moon)," "Medley: a) Hold Me Tight, b) Lazy Dynamite, c) Hands of Love, d) Power Cut," "I Lie Around"*, "Country Dreamer"*, "The Mess"*

Red Rose Speedway rose to number one on the American charts, and peaked—twice— at number four in Britain

V. RED ROSE SPEEDWAY

The Ides of March, 1973 boded very well indeed for Mr. McCartney. At that time he issued the single "My Love"/"The Mess," the former of which has become one of his classics, and one of the most covered ballads ever. It reached number one in the United States and number seven in Britain, and stands as quintessential McCartney. Schmaltz and sentimentality tempered by creative prowess.

Two months later McCartney released his fourth solo (second with Wings) album, **Red Rose Speedway**. It is his best to date. A consistently good track line-up, though with the exception of "My Love," nothing really leaps out at the listener. The overall sense of quality promised things would continue to get better. McCartney's found new confidence, despite competition from former mate George Harrison, whose **Living in the Material World** scored quite well, as did his single "Give Me Love (Give Me Peace on Earth)."

"[**Red Rose Speedway**] wasn't named after Rose, my housekeeper, to debunk another myth," McCartney clarified at one time. "I remember when we did the album cover, Linda took that photo of me as I sat next to a motor bike with a rose in me mouth all evening, listening to [Stevie Wonder's] **Innervisions** album.

"At one point, while I had some of the tunes going, we were up in Scotland at my sheep farm—which seems very lovely on the postcards, until you get to lambing. But you can't help it if you're sensitive, and there was one lamb we were trying to save. The young ones get out into the weather and collapse from exposure; you find them and bring them in. We stayed up all night and had him in front of the stove, but it was too late and he just died. I wrote a song about it [on the album], 'Little Lamb Dragonfly,' and the line was 'I can help you out, but I can't help you in.' It was very sad, so I wrote my little tribute to him."

He's pointed out, "When 'My Love' came out, John Lennon actually said, 'If only everything was as simple and unaffected as McCartney's new single, then maybe Dean Martin and Jerry Lewis would be reunited with the Marx Brothers.' We were going through a slagging off period with each other, although most of the slagging was coming from him. And he did have Allen Klein at that time whispering in his ear. He called me Engelbert, and Engelbert Humperdinck started getting annoyed at *me*. I said, 'It wasn't me, it was John slagging me off, saying I was sounding like you.' And he said, 'John Lennon would never have said that.' 'Well, I've got news for you, he did.' I also know from Yoko that John had sat down in other moments and sort of cried over that stuff. Now I don't know if it was out of sheer sympathy, but I don't think so. He was an emotional fellow."

June of 1973 brought two significant events for McCartney. First was his television special, **James Paul McCartney**, a variety show that only half-worked, although it did keep him in the public eye. The other was the release of his newest single, "Live and Let Die", the title track from the latest James Bond film. This is fitting as veteran Bond director Peter Hunt recalls the Beatles had been tremendous 007 fans, and there had been talk of trying to get them to do a title track back in the Sixties. The talks never went anywhere.

As it is, "Live and Let Die," which reached number 17 in the United States and

acoustic number for a Bond film. You're following something, so you've got to keep vaguely within the format."

His next single, "Helen Wheels"/ "Country Dreamer" (number 10 in America, 26 in Britain) was released in October. "Helen Wheels" stands out as a bouncy little tune, inspired by McCartney's land rover.

"That song described a trip down the M6, which is the big motorway to get from Scotland down to England," he's explained, "so that song was my attempt to put England on the map. All the Chuck Berry songs you ever heard always had things like 'Birmingham, Alabama!' shouted out. These American places like 'Tallahassee!' But you couldn't put English ones in. It always sounded daft to us, 'Scuntharpe!' 'Warrington!' It doesn't sound as funky."

seven in Britain, perfectly encapsulates the world of 007. It stands out among Bond themes as one of the best. Incidentally, the single (as well as the film's soundtrack) was produced by George Martin, marking the first reunion between the two since **Abbey Road**. The combination was magic, just as it had always been.

McCartney said, "When I was asked to do a Bond film, I thought, 'Why not?' I said, 'Look, give me a week. If I can't do it, I'll back out of it.' I don't normally write to titles, but read the Bond book the next day. I was ready to go with George Martin the next week. I found it came easily. I sort of wrote it, got George round to my house, sat down at the piano, worked out an arrangement with him, then he went off and scored it. It was quite easy to do, and turned out well for the film. [The production was big] because of Bond. I didn't feel that I could go and do a little

That same year brought album releases from John Lennon (**Mind Games**) and Ringo Starr (**Ringo**), both well received. Ringo's effort featured contributions from Lennon, Harrison and McCartney, thus coming closest to a Beatles reunion.

1973 was a banner year for Paul McCartney, but the best was still to come.

38

Band on the Run Album Tracks: "Band on the Run," "Jet," "Bluebird," "Mrs. Vanderbilt," "Let Me Roll It," "Mamunia," "No Words," "Helen Wheels"*, "Picasso's Last Words (Drink to Me)", "Nineteen Hundred and Eighty Five"
*On the American release of the al-

Band on the Run reached the number one position in both America and Britain, and sold over eleven million copies around the world, a staggering figure for the time

If early 1973 had been an upswing for Paul McCartney and Wings, **Band on the Run**, released on November 30th in Britain and December 5th in America, showed the best was yet to come. This album topped the American charts on four separate occasions, a feat without precedent.

Wings had experienced a lot that year; a highly successful tour of Britain; the singles "Hi, Hi, Hi," "Live and Let Die," "My Love" and "Helen Wheels" (included on the American version of **Band on the Run** at Capital's insistence); respectable critical reaction to **Red Rose Speedway** and the **James Paul McCartney** television special.

McCartney had already begun writing tracks for his next album, planned for production in Lagos, Africa.

"I thought it would be good to get out of the country to record," he's said, "just for a change. Sometimes you get bored, and think, 'I'm going to the same studio every day,' and you think it will make your album boring. So I had a few ideas for songs that I wanted to do that I was keen on, like 'Band on the Run,' 'Jet' and a few others. I asked EMI where they had studios around the world, and they sent me over a note which listed them, including Rio De Jenario, China and all these amazing countries. Also on the list was Lagos and Nigeria, and I said, 'Lagos, yeah, that's it.' [It] sounded great: Africa, rhythms, percussionists. On that basis, without knowing anything more about it, we went off."

Before Wings flew off a major snag in their plans developed when Henry McCullough and Danny Seiwell quit the band.

"Henry left over what we call 'musical differences,'" McCartney has recounted. "Actually, it *was* a musical difference. We were rehearsing, I asked him to play a certain bit, he was loath to play it, and kind of made an excuse about it 'couldn't be played.' Being a bit of a guitarist myself, I knew it *could* be played. Rather than let it pass, I decided to confront him with it. He decided to confront me with it and we had a confrontation. We both left rehearsals a bit choked. He rang up to say, 'I'm leaving you.'

"And Denny didn't want to come to Africa. That was his thing. Apparently someone had been to his house and made him very nervous about Africa, and he just rang me up and said, 'I can't make this trip, man.' Your jaw kind of hits the ground, and you go, 'Ohhh, dear me.' And it was like I was left in a lurch at the last minute—with literally an hour before we got in the plane to go on this trip to Africa to record. We didn't know what the hell was in store. But that was my first hint of something weird happening here. So we ended up just the three of us in Lagos. Actually, it was good, because it meant I could play drums—or that we were *stuck* with me as the drummer, depending on your outlook. I've just gotta be simple in my playing, because I can't be complicated. Fleetwood Mac-style is my kind of drumming: dead straight, right down to strapping.!"

McCartney's prediction that the departure of two band members foretold things to come proved right on the money. Upon setting foot in Lagos they found the EMI studio was not completely built yet (although they would eventually record there).

41

McCartney: 20 Years on His Own

In addition, McCartney passed out due to "bronchial spasms," he and Linda were mugged and African musicians claimed Wings had come to Lagos to steal their music (a charge McCartney refuted by playing them the music that had been composed thus far). As if that wasn't enough, they all found themselves in the midst of the monsoon season.

"Still," McCartney's mused, "out of the adversity came one of our better albums. [Friction] helped a bit on that one. It gave us [something] to really fight against. We were going uphill all the way."

There's no doubt that **Band on the Run** paid off when it reached record stores towards the end of the year. It was hailed as McCartney's masterpiece; his most consistently powerful post-Beatles album up until that time. It's packed with an incredible line-up of tracks.

Escape. Freedom. Soaring. Eluding.

These words come to mind when listening to the album, beginning with the title track itself. It can certainly be ranked among McCartney's best compositions. The track sounds like three separate songs magically welded together into one thematic motif, perfectly encapsulating the rest of the album.

"There is a thread, but it's not a concept album," McCartney, the brains behind the Sgt. Pepper persona the Beatles took on in the Sixties, has explained. "It sort of relates to me escaping. Most bands on tour are bands on the run. There were a lot of musicians at the time who'd come out of ordinary suburbs in the Sixties and Seventies, and were getting busted. Bands like the Byrds and the Eagles—the mood amongst them was one of desperados. We were being outlawed for pot. It put us on the wrong side of the law. And our argument on the title song was, 'Don't put us on the wrong side, you'll make us into criminals. We're *not* criminals, we don't want to be.' We just would rather do this than hit the booze—which had been the traditional

way to do it. We felt that this was a better move; we had all our theories. I just made up a story about people breaking out of prison. Structurally, that very tight little intro on 'Band on the Run'— 'Stuck inside these four walls'—led to a hole being blasted in the wall and we get the big orchestra and then we're off. We escape into the sun."

The album cover symbolizes the material within. It features Wings with a variety of "personalities" making an obvious prison break, but caught in a spotlight. The personalities are TV interviewer Michael Parkinson, singer Kenny Lynch, actors James Coburn and Christopher Lee, Parliament member Clement Freud and boxer John Conteh.

"'Band on the Run' worked out well as a track," McCartney explained. "Then I think we started toying with the idea of an obvious cover with a band on the run, which would be a bunch of prisoners who'd escaped. But it was Linda who said, 'If we're going to have a bunch of people, instead of just having a bunch of models, wouldn't it be great if each one of them was a face you recognized?' So we got their phone numbers, literally called them up and said, 'Do you fancy it?' Got 'em all down to where the shoot was going to be, stuck some prisoner gear on them and took the photo. It looked like we had been caught, and it was perfect."

The next track was "Jet," one of McCartney's better efforts, a rocker that takes off performed live, as evidenced by the 1976 Wings world tour. "Bluebird" is a wonderful ballad ala "Blackbird," from **The Beatles** (better known as **The White Album**). "Mrs. Vanderbilt", plays as a successful semi-rocker, and "Let Me Roll It", appears to be a musical salute to John Lennon. The vocal is performed very much in the Lennon mode, although McCartney has denied this. "I still don't think it sounds like him, but that's your opinion," he responded to one journalist. "I can dig it if it sounds that way to you."

The remainder of the album, consisting

42

McCartney: 20 Years on His Own

of "Mamunia," "No Words" (co-written by McCartney and Denny Laine), "Helen Wheels," "Picasso's Last Words" and "Nineteen Hundred and Eighty Five" are all consistently good. They demonstrate how far McCartney's songwriting ability had recharged itself. He was now ready to take on anything from the musical legacy he left behind with the Beatles. Of the tracks, "Picasso's Last Words" carries the most interesting story.

The McCartneys had been in Jamaica at the time Steve McQueen and Dustin Hoffman shot sequences for their prison flick, *Papillon*. The rockers got together with Hoffman, and established instant rapport.

"Dustin was saying he thought it was an incredible gift to be able to write a song about something," McCartney told *Rolling Stone*. "People think that, but I always maintain it's the same as any gift. It probably is more magical because it's music...but take his acting talent. It's great. I was saying it's the same as you and acting, when the man says 'Action!' you just pull it out of the bag, don't you? You don't know where it comes from, you just do it. How do you get all of your characterizations? It's just in you. The same with me. With a song, I just pull it out of the air. I knock a couple of chords off, and it suggests a melody to me. If I haven't heard the melody before, I'll keep it."

Amazed, wanting proof of the validity of McCartney's claim, Hoffman brought him an article which stated Picasso's last words were supposedly "Drink to me, drink to my health, you know I can't drink any more," and asked McCartney to put it to music.

"I happened to have my guitar with me," he picked up the scenario, "I'd brought it around and I said, yeah, sure. I strummed a couple of chords I knew I couldn't go wrong on, and started singing, 'Drink to me, drink to my health,' and he leaps out of his chair and says, 'Annie! Annie!' That's his wife. He says, 'The most incredible thing! He's doing it! He's writing it! It's coming out!' He's leaping up and down, just like in the films, you know. And I'm

knocked out because he's so appreciative. I was writing the tune there and he was well chuffed.

"I love the album," McCartney added. "When you make an album, you're waiting for everyone to criticize, waiting for everyone to put it down. You're living on your nerves, really, for the first couple of weeks, wondering if it's going to be the biggest blow-out of all time, or whether it's going to be as good as you think it is. Having listened to it last night for the first time in a couple of weeks and having forgotten it almost, I must say it's great. I love it."

And so, obviously, did the record buying public and the critics. The album's sales, and those of the singles it inspired beginning with "Jet"/"Let Me Roll It" (number seven in America, number six in Britain) on February 14, 1974. The single is credited with bringing the album back to the number one position in the charts. Next up was the coupling of "Band on the Run" and "Nineteen Hundred and Eighty Five" in America on April 8, 1974 (which reached number one, as did the album for a third time), while in Britain the title track was coupled with "Zoo Gang," reaching number three on the charts.

Album Tracks: "Venus and Mars," "Rock Show," "Love in Song," "You Gave Me the Answer," "Magneto and Titanium Man," "Letting Go," "Venus and Mars Reprise," "Spirits of Ancient Egypt," "Medicine Jar," "Call Me Back Again," "Listen to What the Man Said," "Treat Her Gently—Lonely Old People," "Crossroads," "Zoo Gang"*, "Lunchbox/Odd Sox"*, "My Carnival"*
* Denotes singles added to compact disc release

Venus and Mars reached the

number one chart position in both

the American and British charts

VII. VENUS AND MARS

With the success of **Band on the Run** resounding in his ears, Paul McCartney set about the task of finding replacements for the departed members of Wings. He found them in guitarist Jimmy McCulloch and drummer Geoff Britten. With this new line-up in place, the band proceeded to Nashville to shoot a documentary film about the group called **One Hand Clapping**. The film has never been commercially released and is obtainable only on bootleg discs and videos. While there they recorded two singles, "Walking in the Park With Eloise"/"Bridge Over the River Suit," a pair of instrumentals which never entered the record charts in either America or Britain. Both can be found on the **Wings at the Speed of Sound** CD, the first track of which was actually written by McCartney's father, James. He recorded it at the suggestion of singer Chet Atkins, who thought it would be a wonderful gesture. Credited to The Country Hams, "Walking in the Park With Eloise," scored nothing on the charts; it was a lovely thought though.

The second single, "Junior's Farm"/"Sally G" was flip-flopped and reissued two months later with the former "B" side now the headliner. It failed to score. In its first incarnation, the single reached number there in America and number 16 in Britain, while the switched version reached number 39 in America and didn't even enter the charts in Britain. Despite this, it should be emphasized that "Junior's Farm" is a terrific rocker, one of McCartney's best. It can be found on the **Wing's Greatest** CD. "Sally G.," can be found on the **Wings at the Speed of Sound** CD. The Country Western tune seems out of place in the McCartney catalog.

On "Junior's Farm," McCartney has explained, "To me, in a way, it was reminiscent of Dylan's 'Ain't Gonna Work on Maggie's Farm No More.' So the idea I thought was we'll have another farm, Macca's farm, and so the idea was to try and get a kind of fantasy about this person, Junior. We recorded it in Nashville, and had a good session on that."

Around the time "Junior's Farm" was released (and **Band on the Run** was still on the charts), McCartney found himself in direct competition with John Lennon's "Whatever Gets You Through The Night"/"Beef Jerky" single and **Walls and Bridges** album, as well as Ringo's "Only You"/"Call Me" single and **Goodnight Vienna** album, and George Harrison's "Ding Dong"/"I Don't Care Anymore" single and **Dark Horse** album. The former Fabs couldn't come close to matching McCartney's critical and commercial success this time. It was quite a turn-around from the outset of the decade.

Wings had begun work on the next album, to be called **Venus and Mars**, at Abbey Road studios in England. They laid down the tracks for "Love in Song," "Letting Go" and "Medicine Jar," and flew to New Orleans to finish. Unfortunately, personality clashes within the group resulted in the exit of drummer Geoff Britten, who was replaced by Joe English, an American. While album sessions were being completed, plans were laid for a world tour. McCartney and company would finally go to the United States.

The next single from the band was "Listen to What the Man Said"/"Love in Song" (number one in America, number six in Britain), issued in May of 1975, seven months after their last. Both highly effective tracks were culled from a forth-

'I think that's it.' He said, 'Did you record that?' I said, 'Yes,' and we listened to it back. No one could believe it, so he went out and tried a few more, but they weren't as good. He'd had all the feel on his early take, the first take. So we'd finished the session. I think that his playing on that song is lovely and that, overall, it worked."

coming LP, with "Listen to What the Man Said" proving one of McCartney's strongest numbers.

Explaining the song, McCartney's noted, "To me, I'm saying, listen to the base rules, don't goof off too much. If you say 'The Man,' it could mean God, it could mean women listen to your men, it could mean many things. It's a good summer single. There's a funny story about that one. It was one of the songs we'd gone in with high hopes for. Whenever I would play it on the piano, people would say, 'Oh, I like that one.' But when we did the backing track, we thought we didn't really get it together at all. We let it stay and added some things on it. Dave Mason came in and we did a little bit of over-dubbing guitars, and then we wondered what we could do for a solo. We thought it would be great to have a very technical musician come in and do a great lyrical solo. Someone said 'Tom Scott lives near here,' [we called] and he turned up within half an hour. There he was, with his sax, and he sat down in the studio playing through. The engineer recording it. We kept all the notes he was playing casually. He came in and I said,

In late May, **Venus and Mars** was released as an effective follow-up to **Band on the Run**. It marked a slight step down in overall lyrical quality. Still, quite a few gems, including the title track, its reprise, and "Rock Show," seem to have been tailor-made for touring. "Magneto and Titanium Man," a salute to Marvel Comics characters is whimsical fun; "Letting Go," is an intense little rocker and "Spirits of Ancient Egypt" offers a terrific Denny Laine lead vocal. "Medicine Jar," an interesting rocker written and sung by guitarist Jimmy McCulloch, served as a prophetic statement regarding his future (he was destined to die of a drug overdose in 1979, after leaving the band). And, of course, "Listen to What the Man Said." Seven out of twelve, not a bad ratio.

Over the years, McCartney recalled many of the tracks featured on this album, noting, "The song 'Venus and Mars' is about an imaginary friend who's got a girl friend who's into astrology, the kind of person who asks you what your sign is before they say hello. I didn't know they were neighboring planets. I just thought of naming any two planets. What were the first that came to mind? I thought, 'Jupiter, no, that doesn't fit...Saturn....no....Venus and Mars....that's great, I'll put those in.' Later, it turns out they've just done an eclipse, Venus and Mars have lined themselves up for the first time in something like a thousand years. I didn't know they were the gods of love and war, either.

"I've been reading a bit of science fiction, things like *Foundation* by Asimov. I love the scope of it, the vision of it, because you can write anything. The second time 'Venus and Mars' comes around, it says, 'Sitting in the hall of the Great Cathedral/Waiting for the transport to come.' That's like in science fiction books, waiting for the space shuttle. 'Starship 2iZNA9,' that's the kind of thing you'll find in Asimov. I like that, sitting in the Cathedral, really waiting for the saucer to come down, to take him off to Venus and Mars or whatever.'"

"Rock Show," he says, was *not* necessarily done for use in touring, but used words that rhymed and fit the motif of the track. "Often these things that turn out to be great afterwards are just searches for a rhyme. I could see how you might think, well, he's doing this...but for me, it's just writing a song."

A track that McCartney enjoyed was "You Gave Me the Answer," a song done in the mode of "When I'm 64," "Honey Pie" and "Your Mother Should Know." In response to criticism levelled against the track's inclusion, he said, "I know it's sort of a rock-and-roll album, but there's other things I like that aren't necessarily rock-and-roll. On this LP, I thought I'd like to get some of that in, so 'You Gave Me the Answer' is real fruity, imagining ties and tails, my impression of the Fred Astaire era. You have to remember when people of my generation were growing up, rock and roll hadn't been invented yet. Blues had started, but that was nowhere near as popular; you had to be a real folkie to be into blues.

Anything up to the 1950s was the old traditions, and in Britain that was music hall, or vaudeville. My dad, sitting around the house tapping out things like 'Chicago' on the ivories, used to get told off by his dad for playing what his dad called 'tin can music.'"

Regarding "Magneto and Titanium Man," McCartney has said, "That's about Marvel comics. When we were on holiday in Jamaica, we'd go into the supermarket every Saturday, when they got a new stack of comics in. I didn't use to read comics from eleven onwards. I thought I'd grown out of them, but I came back to them a couple of years ago. The drawings are neat. I think you'll find that in twenty years time some of the guys drawing them were little Picassos. I think it's very clever how they do it. I love the names, I love the whole comic book thing.

"I also liked 'Letting Go' and then there was 'Medicine Jar', written by the late Wings guitarist Jimmy McCulloch and his friend Colin Allen from Stone the Crows. Jimmy wanted to write an anti-drug song. As to *why* he wanted to, I'm not sure, but I'd say he'd seen the personal warning signs. That song, I think, was Jimmy talking to himself. Listening to it now and knowing the circumstances of how he died, I'm sure that's what it is. He's really saying to himself, 'Get your hand out of the medicine jar.' I don't think he managed to. He was a great guitar player, but he was into a little too much heavy stuff. But if I'm reading into it, then let's just say I'm as bad as the critics, okay?"

In September of 1975, "Letting Go"/ "You Gave Me the Answer" saw release as a single (number 39 in America, it didn't even enter the top 30 in Britain), followed in November by "Venus and Mars—Rock Show"/ "Magneto and Titanium Man" (number 12 in America, it didn't hit the chart in Britain).

In light of the previous two years, these relative failures didn't affect McCartney. Wings was hot. Audiences around the world lined up for the group's tour.

Wings at the Speed of Sound Album Tracks: "Let 'Em In," "The Note You Never Wrote," "She's My Baby," "Beware My Love," "Wino Junko," "Silly Love Songs," "Cook of the House," "Time to Hide," "Must Do Something About It," "San Ferry Anne," "Warm and Beautiful," "Walking in the Park With Eloise"*, "Bridge on the River Suite"*, "Sally G."*
*Denotes singles added to compact disc release

Wings at the Speed of Sound

made it to number one on the

American charts, and made it as

high as number two in Britain

VIII. WINGS AT THE SPEED OF SOUND

Between the British, Australian and American tour dates [see next section], Wings had the opportunity to go into the studio and cut **Wings at the Speed of Sound**, the weakest album since **Band on the Run**. Despite some first rate compositions (i.e. "Let 'Em In", "Beware My Love" and "Silly Love Songs"), the album seems disjointed, with no central theme unifying the tracks. The songs have lost the harder edge of the previous two efforts. If the listener was pressed to find a theme, arguably it deals with things domestic, tranquility in the home. Domestic bliss is undoubtedly as important to Paul McCartney as it is to any of us, but in terms of riveting music? It just doesn't fit in with what Wings had most recently delivered.

It does allow Wings to be what McCartney had always claimed it was: a *group*, as opposed to a backing band for him. Denny Laine sings lead vocal on McCartney's "The Note You Never Wrote," Linda McCartney sings lead vocal on his "Cook of the House" as does Joe English on "Must Do Something About It," all three handling the task just fine.

This album caused the critics to turn a hundred and eighty degrees in terms of adulation of Paul McCartney. In 1973 he had once again become the golden child, a moniker he kept through his tour of America in 1976, but now the tide was changing again. Many of the tracks on **Wings at the Speed of Sound** were dismissed as light fluff, and the critical appraisal would stick through the next couple of albums. Yet this didn't bother McCartney as the lyrics of some of the tracks, particularly "Silly Love Songs," addressed this straight on.

"Some people want to fill the world with Silly Love Songs, and what's wrong with that?" he sings, emphasizing—critics be damned—that this is what he does, and that the public enjoys it. So why can't they? Subsequent criticisms of this song were not easy to brush off.

"I *liked* the song," he told *Rolling Stone*, "but I listen to people and I just get *crackers*. All someone has to say is, 'A bit poppy,' or 'That was a bit sickly, that one,' and I expect the song to flop. Someone says, 'It's a bit too cute.' Well, I *know* that. What do you think goes through my mind when I'm writing a song about *silly* love songs? I'm flashing on all of this: 10cc have done a song called 'Silly Love,' so I'm in danger there. The hard nuts of the music business, the critics, are gonna hate because I'm not writing about *acne*.

"You weigh all those problems up and you still write it," he continued. "You *know* all those problems, you don't need somebody to tell you that it doesn't cook or whatever the critics are going to tell you. Unfortunately, it still tends to get to me. I still hear them saying it's no good. I wonder if they're right. I wonder if I'm right. And it's great when something wins a poll and you can say, 'Nyahh, nuts to you. I thought I was right.' It's a vindication."

Overall, McCartney enjoyed the album and was proud of it, "We fit [the album] in. We had a great holiday in Hawaii and I got the album together there in my head. We started recording it in January—or February, I'm a bit hazy. The album didn't take long. But we didn't rush it—just let the ideas blossom. We [tried] to make it as hard as possible, but sometimes you just don't bring off in a studio what you can bring off in a live thing.

"There were a few things I especially wanted to do," he told one journalist. "I put a backing track down and then got the idea of getting Joe English to do it, because he's got a very good voice. Linda's got this track called 'Cook of the House,' so I thought it would be good to give one to Joe. When he'd done it, we were all surprised. He sings well. The band came together for rehearsals at Elstree and a nice thing was the way the brass players worked out a bit for a song called 'Silly Love Songs.' They can really get behind it, because it's theirs. We also used two euphoniums on 'Warm and Beautiful.'

"The object with anything I do [is] to try and get out of a rut and do something different. When I was in Jamaica, I heard a reggae record which featured a trombone all on its own. It sounded daft and fruity and I filed it away in the back of my mind that I'd love to use a trombone. And of course, now we have Tony Dorsey, who plays trombone for us, so we could use it as a solo instrument on the album."

In regards to "Let 'Em In", McCartney noted, "It seemed a good introduction to the album. I don't think of particular themes for an album. There wasn't one on **Venus and Mars**. I thought of a bunch of tunes. They have a sort of family, loveish, warmish feel. Well...I can never analyze me own stuff. I hope the reviewers like it, but if they don't, I hope the people like it."

They did, judging by the album's sales [see sidebar], bolstered by the single release in April 1976 of "Silly Love Songs"/"Cook of the House." The single reached number one in both America and Britain. This must have been good news to Wings in the midst of their tour of America.

July saw the second single release from **Wings at the Speed of Sound**, "Let 'Em In"/"Beware My Love," which reached number three in America and number two in Britain, thus driving home the point that with or without the critics, Wings had touched a chord with its audience.

50

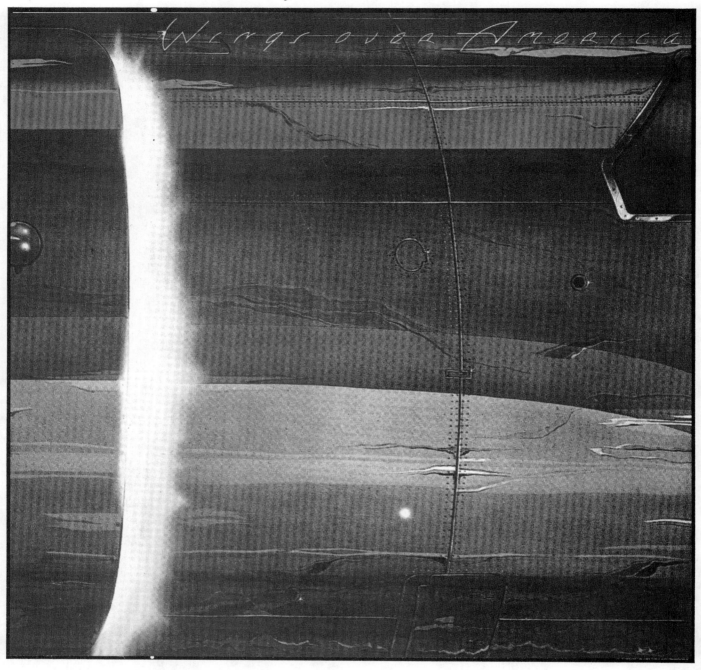

Wings Over America Album Tracks: "Venus and Mars," "Rock Show," "Jet," "Let Me Roll It," "Spirits of Ancient Egypt," "Medicine Jar," "Maybe I'm Amazed," "Call Me Back Again," "Lady Madonna," "The Long and Winding Road," "Live and Let Die," "Picasso's Last Words," "Richard Cory," "Bluebird," "I've Just Seen a Face," "Blackbird," "Yesterday," "You Gave Me the Answer," "Magneto and Titanium Man," "Go Now," "My Love," "Listen to What the Man Said," "Let 'Em In," "Time to Hide," "Silly Love Songs," "Beware My Love," "Letting Go," "Band on the Run," "Hi Hi Hi," "Soily"

Wings Over America reached number one in America while it peaked at number five in Britain

IX. WINGS OVER AMERICA

By the time he was ready for a world tour, Paul McCartney felt confident enough to include a handful of Beatles tunes in Wings' repertoire, appealing to older fans while attracting new ones.

"In the Sixties," he said, "or the main Beatle time, there was screaming all the time. And I liked that then because that was that kind of time. I used to feel that that was kind of like a football match. They came just to cheer; the cheering turned into screaming when it translated into young girls. People used to say, 'Well, isn't that a drag, 'cause no one listens to your music.' But some of the time it was good they didn't, because...you know, some of the time we were playing pretty rough there, as almost any band from that time will know. I thought when I came out on tour again, it might be very embarrassing if they were listening instead of screaming.

"David Essex was talking excitedly about the British audience, 'They're still screaming, you know.' Well, for *him* they are, and that's his kind of audience, but when we went out, we just got up there and started playing like we were a new group. So everyone just took us like that. Sat there. 'Yeah, that's all right.' And they got up and danced when we did dancing numbers. It's perfect: you can have your cake and eat it, because they roar when you need them to roar and they listen when you're hoping they might be listening.

"There is this feeling that I should mind if they come to see me as a Beatle. But I really don't mind. They're coming to see me; I don't knock it. It doesn't matter why they came, it's what they think when they go home. I don't know for sure, but I've got a feeling that they go away thinking, 'Oh well, it's a band.' It lets them catch up. I think the press, the media, is a bit behind the times, thinking about the Beatles a lot. And I think the kids go away from the show a lot hipper than even the review they're going to read the next day."

The tour began in Britain on September 9, 1975 and ran until the 23rd. Audiences went absolutely wild over Paul McCartney and Wings, raving that Macca had finally come into his own. There was no longer any question he had moved far beyond the confines of the legend of the Beatles. The press, too, loved the shows, as noted by the review which ran in *The London Times* regarding a performance at Wembley. "Paul McCartney," wrote journalist Clive Bennett, "is surely the most gifted songwriter of the post-war period. No one else captures so expressively the vulnerability of new love or so poignantly the loneliness in our society. He is no less successful using pulsating rock rhythms to express happiness. When his talent is coupled to a real performing skill, the result is, and last night was, unstoppable.

"McCartney and his band Wings....have polished their lighting and stage effects to a rare pitch of excellence and their simple performance style follows suit.

"Despite its familiarity, they showed no signs of boredom with their set. In any case, it was too inventive and the audience response too positive for there to be much danger of that. Most of the songs came from McCartney's post-Beatles days, though there was a sprinkling of the older numbers. Significantly, two he performed in his solo spot, 'Blackbird' and especially 'Yesterday,' came from that period and received the loudest applause, and the first piece really to get the audience going was another, 'Lady Madonna.'

"The set was in two parts. The first opened with McCartney appearing Apollo-like from a cloud of dry ice, descending bubbles and simple but effective lighting. It reached a climax ten songs later with 'Live and Let Die,' the stage shrouded in a mass of perfectly timed smoke bombs seared by a laser beam. After the applause, the band took up their acoustic instruments for a selection of simpler songs before a return to electrical instruments and a scintillating version of 'You Gave Me the Answer.'

"A word of praise for the members of the band. All of them took their solo spots as expected, but the extra highlight was in the backing brass quartet and especially Tony Dorsey, the trombonist."

The tour of Britain over, Wings took off for Australia in October with the intention of following up with a tour of Japan, but were denied entrance to the country due to a previous arrest of McCartney for possession of pot. With Japan out of the running, McCartney focused his energies on the upcoming shows in America. They would subsequently be delayed from their scheduled April 8, 1976 debut to May 3 due to the death of McCartney's father and guitarist Jimmy McCulloch fracturing his pinky.

When they finally arrived, it was one hell of a reception as latter day Beatlemania swept the nation. American teenagers had discovered the Beatles for the first time when Capital issued the **Rock and Roll** compilation album (number two in America, number ten in Britain) and twenty three singles, one of which, "Yesterday," reached number five on the British charts. Another, "Got to Get You Into My Life," reached number three in America. No small feat for a band that had disbanded six years earlier!

Rather than feeling threatened by this turn of events, McCartney was de-lighted; many of those swept up in the renewed Beatlemania had discovered it only after falling for Paul McCartney's band Wings! McCartney had come a long way since 1970 when many doubted he would find life after the Beatles.

"Everything I have done since the Beatles split has been leading up to this [tour]," he said at the time. "I would have said if you asked me in 1969 if a group could have done it after the Beatles; if any of the Beatles could have had the strength to actually do something else, because it's a hell of a thing when you've been in one group all your life. I would have bet you then there was no chance of getting Wings going. All these silly little university tours and getting Linda in. I mean, I thought, 'This is gonna flop, this is just gonna be mad, this whole thing is just silly.' But it doesn't seem to be. It's nice. Somehow it's got a chemistry that manages to hang it all together."

Between May 9, 1976 and June 23, Wings played twenty one cities with a total of thirty one performances. They received the kind of rave reviews that had greeted the band in Britain and elsewhere. *Newsweek* magazine noted, "After his first American concert in ten years, Paul McCartney was flushed and triumphant. It had been six years since the breakup of the Beatles, and the audience in Forth Worth, Texas had just given the former Beatle and his band, Wings, a screaming ovation. Paul McCartney had proved that he could make it on his own.

"[The tour] is elaborately designed to solidify McCartney's new musical identity with Wings. For two hours and fifteen minutes, McCartney and his hard-driving band put on a tightly wound, skillfully paced show that capitalized on showbiz effects ranging from lasers and green smoke projected over the audience to a giant backdrop of a David Hockney painting. Although McCartney is careful to share the spotlight with Wings, he's the main attraction.

"Driving Wings through twenty nine songs, including five Beatles hits,

McCartney still looks like a naughty choirboy. He not only plays his famous left-handed bass, but is strong on the piano as well. In a solo moment, he revives the old Beatles magic by singing 'Yesterday,' and he acknowledges the cheers with an exuberant salute to the crowd and thumbs-up signal."

For those who did not experience the tour first hand, two examples best convey the experience of that historic moment. The video cassette of **Rock Show**, a visual recording of one entire show, and the two-disc CD of **Wings Over America**, effortlessly capture the excitement of the moment. The CD preserves the magic better than the video! With the right stereo equipment, you can close your eyes and experience the show first hand.

"I feel now there's as much good music as there ever was," McCartney confidently noted in the midst of the tour. "It's a bit of a drag to have been a legend, but it's also a bit of a drag to have to leave it and say, 'Well, folks, I'm thirty three now and past it.' I don't feel past it now in any way. I feel with this band, we've only just begun."

Paul McCartney was justifiably proud of his renewed stature in the music world, having accomplished the goal he had set for himself some six years earlier. Lightning had been re-captured in a bottle. He had once again started from nothing and moved on to world domination of the music industry.

One question remained: Where could he go from there?

London Town Album Tracks: "London Town," "Cafe on the Left Bank," "I'm Carrying," "Backwards Traveller," "Cuff Link," "Children Children," "Girlfriend," "I've Had Enough," "With A Little Luck," "Famous Groupies," "Deliver Your Children," "Name and Address," "Don't Let It Bring You Down," "Morse Moose and the Grey Goose," "Girl's School"*
* Denotes single added to compact disc release

London Town was a tremendous hit in America, reaching number two on the charts, while it climbed to number four in Britain

X. LONDON TOWN

In the 1960s, one sign of success for the Beatles was "conquering" the world on a tour that smashed all previous records. They followed with a second, more mechanical tour, then retired to the studio to do what they did best, evolve musically, and bring the listener along for the ride.

With the phenomenon surrounding the Wings world tour, Paul McCartney wanted history to repeat itself. But first, because both **Wings at the Speed of Sound** and **Wings Over America** were achieving tremendous sales, he ran with the momentum by issuing the live single "Maybe I'm Amazed"/"Soily" (number ten in America, number twenty seven in Britain) in January of 1977. The former sounded even better than the original version, the live performance adding a certain sense of power to the lyrics, while the second works wonderfully as a rocker.

Several months later saw the oddest McCartney release of all, an album called **Thrillington**, an orchestral version of **Ram**. The disc is credited to one Percy "Thrills" Thrillington, reportedly a pseudonym for McCartney.

"Well, you always see these albums like *James Last Does Tchaikovsky* or *Nelson Riddle Plays Mantovani*," he told *Musician* magazine. "I thought it'd be amusing to have your own tunes from an album and take them to the middle of the road as a mischievous way to infiltrate the light TV programs and things that use such fluff. It was another silly idea along the way, but we scoured the world for orchestra leader Percy 'Thrills' Thrillington..." at which point he supposedly winked at his interviewer, "...Finally found him in Ireland! He and a friend of his did some arrangements and laid this album. Now, I think it should all have been done up *louder*!"

Needless to say, **Thrillington** had absolutely no impact on the record charts anywhere!

The next single, released on November 11, 1977, was "Mull of Kintyre"/"Girl's School," the latter a terrific little rocker. The former, however, much like the previous Wings effort "Give Ireland Back to the Irish," was difficult for an American to appreciate. "Mull of Kintyre," which only reached number thirty three in America, was a smashing number one hit in Britain with over two million units sold, replacing the Beatles' "She Loves You" as that country's number one single. Co-written by Denny Laine, the song refers to an area on the Scottish peninsula.

"We thought it should be a single and it sounds very Christmasy and New Yeary," McCartney has noted. "It's a kind of glass of ale in your hand, leaning up against the bar tune. We had the local pipe band join in and we took a mobile studio up to Scotland and put the equipment in an old barn. We had the Cambeltown Band and they were great—just pipes and drums. It was interesting, writing for them. You can't just write any old tune. They can't play every note in a normal scale. They've got the drone going all the time, so you have to be careful what chord you change over the drone. So it's a very simple song. I had to conduct them very heavily. It's a waltz and an attempt at writing a new Scottish tune. All the other Scottish tunes are old traditional stuff, and I like bagpipes anyway."

Prior to the release of the single, Wings had set upon the task of recording its next

album, **London Town**. The word "task" may not be an appropriate one, as much of it was done at sea. Some recordings had been done at EMI's Abbey Road studios between early February and late March of 1977, but the majority was cut aboard a yacht called the *Fair Carol*, on which a twenty four track studio was installed.

"We went to London to start the album in our normal way," McCartney explained. "But it was cloudy old London, and our engineer, Geoff Emerick, started telling us tales of how he'd been recording in Hawaii. Everyone started feeling extremely jealous. We realized we'd worked in Abbey Road for a long time. It all fell into place. We thought about the boat and doing something in the Virgin Islands. So we ended up on a boat called the *Fair Carol*, and just spent a bit of time there.

"We wanted to create a situation that would take the sweat out of work. I hate the grind of trying to seek inspiration. The studio worked out incredibly well and the very first day we got a track down. There was a nice free feeling. We'd swim in the day and record at night. We had written most of the songs beforehand. We stayed a month on the boat, and by the time we recorded it, the songs just seemed to work. It's nice work, if you can get it."

Unfortunately Jimmy McCulloch and Joe English both quit Wings.

McCartney explained, "[They] did all their stuff before they split. They were on the boat and then Denny and I finished off the album. A couple of years ago I used to worry if anyone left—'Oh God, I can't keep a group together.' But now I don't worry. There is no need to keep it together all the time. I'm more interested in the music and if we can do that, I don't mind how it has to be done."

The first single from **London Town**, "With a Little Luck"/"Backwards Traveller/Cuff Link," was released on March 23rd, 1978 and scored a tremendous hit, reaching number one in America and number seven in Britain. These tracks were among the best from the forthcoming album, although very much in the **Wings at the Speed of Sound** vein. "With a Little Luck" is a wistful number that sounds as though it could have come from any number of latter day Beatles albums, while "Backwards Traveller/Cuff Link" is the kind of throwaway rocker McCartney is so good at. The lyrics may not say much, but the song as a whole captures the listener.

London Town is a tough album to assess; it's certainly pleasant to listen to, but it sounds even lighter than its predecessor. Some tracks stand out—the aforementioned numbers as well as "London Town," "I've Had Enough" and "Famous Groupies"— but on the whole it doesn't have the lasting impact of a **Band on the Run** or **Venus and Mars**. There's no doubt McCartney gave his all, but it seems he lacked a tangible goal, and that is something he needs to excel.

June 16th saw the release of "I've Had Enough"/"Deliver Your Children," which only reached number twenty five on the American charts, and couldn't climb above forty five in Britain. It was quite a letdown from "With a Little Luck," but McCartney remained philosophical. "You can't win 'em all," he said. "Just didn't mean anything to people, I suppose. I can't pick 'em, but I'm very lucky. Out of all the ones I've released, quite a number of them have been hits, so I'm thankful for small murphies."

Next up was the August 26th single release of "London Town"/"I'm Carrying," which fared even worse, not even entering the top thirty in America or Britain.

Something strange seemed to be happening. One question began popping up frequently: had McCartney lost touch with his audience?

XI. WING'S GREATEST OR "TAKING IT EASY"

Wings Greatest Album Tracks: "Another Day," "Silly Love Songs," "Live and Let Die," "Junior's Farm," "With a Little Luck", "Band on the Run", "Uncle Albert/Admiral Halsey," "Hi Hi Hi," "Let 'Em In," "My Love," "Jet," "Mull of Kintyre"

Despite the fact that it didn't sell well (number twenty nine in America and number three in Britain), Wings Greatest is a terrific compilation album, emphasizing just how far Paul McCartney had come since the break-up of the Beatles in 1970.

Although it bounces around chronologically, the tracks feature McCartney at his best, whether on such lighter numbers as "Silly Love Songs," "My Love" and "With a Little Luck" or all-out rockers like "Junior's Farm," "Jet" and "Band on the Run".

If in 1978 McCartney was indeed taking it easy, this line-up of hits at least gave him a good excuse to do so.

16Back to the Egg Album Tracks: "Reception," "Getting Closer," "We're Open Tonight," "Spin It On," "Again and Again and Again," "Old Siam, Sir," "Arrow Through Me," "rockestra Theme," "To You," "After the Ball/Million Miles," "Winter Rose/Love Awake," "The Broadcast," "So Glad to See You Here," "Baby's Request," "Daytime Nightime Suffering"*, "Wonderful Christmastime"*, "Rudolph the Red Nose Raggae"*
* Denotes singles added to compact disc release

Back to the Egg only reached number eight in America and barely made number four in Br[...]tain, before slipping down the charts

XII. BACK TO THE EGG

In the late Seventies, disco was king, thanks to the phenomenal success of John Travolta's *Saturday Night Fever*. Seeming to capitalize on this trend, Wings released "Goodnight Tonight"/"Daytime Nightime Suffering" on March 23, 1979. A thoroughly effective dance track that reached number five in America and number six in Britain, it introduced guitarist Lawrence Juber and drummer Steve Holly as the newest members of Wings.

"That's the one that put me back on the map with a top ten hit," McCartney reflected recently. "I do like dance records. Some people say, 'Oh, it's a dance record,' as if there's something wrong with it, but basically when you listen to records, you want to dance. We recorded it in a long version, as opposed to stretching it like they do now. I think I got fed up with the remix mechanizing, the dub stuff. I think it'll date very quickly. It's not that I'm following the crowd, but if there's a lot of people into a thing, I generally check it out to see why they all like it. But I didn't plan the timing at all. We had a meeting and decided it would be nice to have a single out, because it had been something like seven months since we'd put a record out. 'Goodnight Tonight' was going to be the B side, and 'Daytime Nightime Suffering' was going to be the A side. So we sat around for years—well, it seemed like years—discussing it, you know, the normal soul-searching you go through. And we decided, 'No, it isn't all right; we won't put it out.' So we scrapped the whole thing. And about a week later I played the record again. I thought, 'That's crazy, we've made it; it's stupid, why not put it out? Just because people are gonna pan it?' I liked it and other people had taken it home and played it to people at parties. So we decided to do it."

On May 24th (June 8th in Britain), **Back to the Egg**, recorded between 1978 and '79 in four different studios in England, was released. Two things immediately became apparent: one, Wings was trying something new, and, two, the experiment didn't quite work. Numbers like "Spin It On", "Old Siam, Sir", "After the Ball" and "Rockestra Theme" are great, but much of the album simply doesn't hold the listener's attention. This is particularly unfortunate in that McCartney had obviously taken recent criticisms of his work to heart, and was attempting a harder, New Wave approach.

Two tracks on the album feature an interesting contrast. "Baby's Request" once again gives us McCartney's sentimental side and is a throwback to the twenties or thirties, while "Rockestra Theme" is kick-ass rock and roll, featuring an all star line-up of musicians including the Who's Pete Townshend, Led Zeppelin's John Bonham and John Paul Jones, and Pink Floyd's David Gilmour.

"It was just where I was at the time," he explained. "The New Wave thing was happening and I was thinking things like, 'Well, a lot of the New Wave is just that they take things at a faster tempo than we do.' 'We' being like what I might call 'Permanent Wave'—joke, number one and the last one—I sort of realized, 'Well, so what's wrong with us doing an uptempo uptempo?' And I get influenced. I always am getting influenced. **Back to the Egg** was influenced just as what I had wanted to do at the time, the direction I felt I hadn't been in for a while—do a bit of that. And the sales, by most other people's standards would be like very healthy.

By our standards, they weren't that good."

And neither were they for the singles spawned from the album either. In Britain, "Old Siam, Sir"/"Spin It On" was issued on June 1st and only made it to number twenty seven on the charts, while "Getting Closer"/"Spin It On," released on June 5th, reached number twenty on the American charts. The next single in Britain, "Getting Closer"/"Baby's Request" was issued on August 10th, but only rose to number sixty, while "Arrow Through Me"/"Old Siam, Sir" made it to twenty nine in America. In an extremely rare occurrence, public and critics alike agreed the album didn't work.

"I'm used to all that by now," said McCartney. "You know nearly everything I've ever done or been involved in has had some of that negative critical reaction. You'd think that something like 'She Loves You' with the Beatles would be pretty positive. But it wasn't. The very first week out, that was supposed to be the worst song the Beatles had ever thought of doing. [But] I don't really feel the need for everything to be incredible and great. I'd probably get quite annoyed if I had a big string of albums that didn't do it, but I'm more interested in the new thing. We went in there thinking it was going to be a good album. But when you've done fifteen albums since the Beatles, they can't all be good. Who is there whose every single album is incredible? I can't think of anyone."

Ironically, Paul McCartney's next "new" thing would be an old friend—himself.

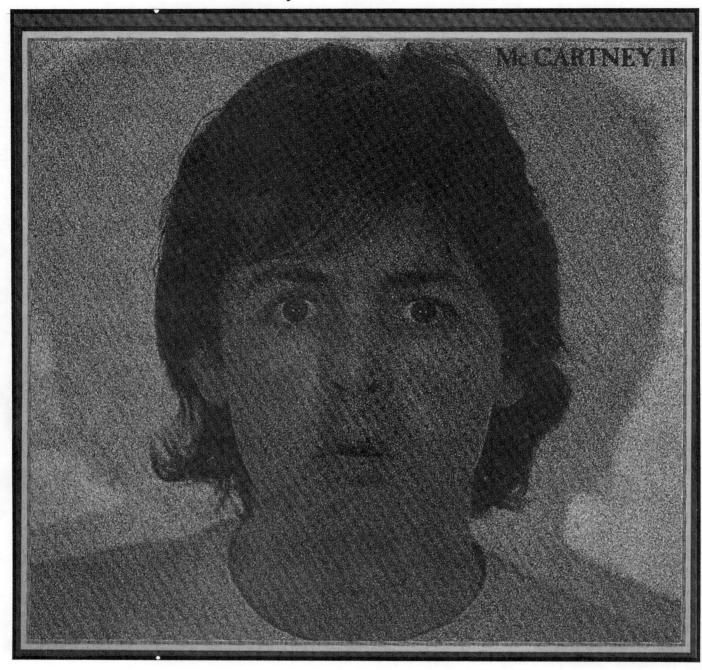

XIII. McCARTNEY II

If
London
Town, Wings Great-
est, Back to the Egg and their
related singles had scored with critics and
public in the same way Band on the Run and Venus and Mars had, Paul McCartney might have given up
touring altogether. Reportedly, though, Denny Laine, in particular,
want to get out of the studio. According to Paul McCartney—The Definitive
Biography, Laine said, "I'm desperate to be on tour. I get twitchy sitting around in
a studio. I am quite sure we will be touring soon, otherwise I honestly feel that I
wouldn't be able to stay in Wings."

McCartney added, "There was one point where we felt we had to be on stage every
night if we were going to be any good. But when it comes around to the right time,
we'll do it—go out and play. We actually fancy playing it in some small, steamy
clubs and get back to the people right there and play to them for a laugh. We keep
wanting to do a residency. We'd like to get a little club somewhere and build an
audience. We'd like to get a great little scene going for a couple of weeks."

McCartney retreated to the plan he had initiated for Wings at the beginning and
had wanted to bring to the Beatles: get back to basics, and build from there. In early 70's, you believed him, but nearly a decade later, it was hard to imagine this artist, who had so successfully captured the world in two musical incarnations, would
do so a third time.

On November 16, 1979, McCartney issued a solo recording, "Wonderful Christmastime"/"Rudolph the Red Nosed Reggae," both included on the Back to the Egg
CD as bonus tracks. An enjoyable number, "Wonderful Christmastime" reached
number sixteen in Britain, but didn't enter the American charts, yet has subsequently become a perennial favorite.

That same month, Wings began a tour of the U.K., destined to be its last. The band
performed eighteen concerts. One source lists the featured songs as "Got to Get
You Into My Life," "My Love," "Getting Closer," "Every Night," "Again and
Again and Again," "I've Had Enough," "Cook of the House," "Old Siam, Sir,"
"Maybe I'm Amazed," "Fool on the Hill," "Let It Be," "Hot as Sun," "Spin It On,"
"Twenty Flight Rock," Laine's "Go Now," "Arrow Through Me," "Wonderful
Christmastime," the forthcoming "Coming Up," "Goodnight Tonight," "Yes-
terday," "Mull of Kintyre" and "Band on the Run."

The shows scored a tremendous success, paving the way for an even more ex-
tensive tour. The second tour marked McCartney's first visit to Japan since his
Beatles days, as he had been denied a visa in 1976 due to having been arrested previously for pot possession. Now the way was finally cleared, but no sooner did
Wings arrive than McCartney was arrested for bringing ninety eight grams of pot
into the country. The tour was cancelled, and McCartney was thrown in jail for ten
days. He must have wondered if he would ever get out; the charges against him
could have resulted in a seven year prison term. Luckily Japanese officials decided
to deport him instead. He and Linda were the last of the entourage to leave, as the
rest of Wings had departed the country earlier.

"The worst thing was the wife and kids; I really lumbered them with the whole
mess. Plus the tour, of course—I had to pay the promoter and everything, which

was an absolutely ridiculous waste. Plus the fans who'd been waiting a long time didn't get to see us. So I was very down the first few days. At first I thought it was barbaric," he's recalled of the experience. "I was woken up at six in the morning then had to sit cross-legged for roll call. It was like Bridge on the River Kwai. They shouted out '22' in Japanese and I had to shout back 'hai.' After a while, though, your natural resilience brings you back. You think, 'Come on. I'm not going down the Black Hole of Calcutta.' You start looking forward to visits, clean shirts, stuff like that."

Upon returning home, McCartney recorded his memories of the experience in long hand for posterity. Then he returned his attention to a solo album he had been working on prior to his arrest.

"In the clink, I had a lot of time to think," he'd said at the time. "I just thought, 'Well, before I do anything else, I want to finish up the solo album.'"

McCartney II, which was released a little more than ten years after his first solo album, featured him on all instruments and vocals. "It was after Back to the Egg and I just had to do something totally different. And so I got this machine and plugged one single microphone into the back of [it] and didn't use a recording console. At the end of the two weeks, I'd done a few tracks. I was starting to get in to it, so I kept it another two weeks and another two weeks and another two weeks. And it just kept coming out. [Originally] I wasn't trying to do an album. In fact, I was trying not to do an album, but in the end I had a few tracks and played it to a couple of people and they said, 'Oh, I see, that's your next album,' and it occurred to me, 'Oh, yeah, it probably is.' So then I got a bit serious on it and tried to make it into an album. That was the worst part of it. I was having fun 'til then.

"The second [solo album] seemed less sophisticated in my mind," he added. 'I don't know whether it is or not. The second one was done not with all the home comforts of the first, but in a der-

elict farm house in the countryside in southern England that was about to be knocked down. I recorded in what had been the front parlor with a tape machine, a couple of sequencers and some amps, bass, guitar and drums. The overriding memory of making that album was that I did some songs in their original versions in about ten minutes, then I'd have to go back and add, say, the maraca part for ten minutes, too. Bloody hell! I'm alone in the middle of the country and it took, like self hypnosis to keep going, shaking the maracas like a baby for about eight minutes."

The first single from these sessions arrived in April, 1980 in the form of Wings' "Coming Up"("Coming Up Live in Glasgow"), "Lunchbox" and "Odd Sox." The latter two appeared on the Venus and Mars CD, and reached number one in America and number two in Britain. A strange little song that fans either love or hate, "Coming Up" has an infectious bounce. The intended single version featured a slightly speeded up vocal and hit big in Britain, while the live version became number one in America.

"I did 'Coming Up' in a reverse way of normal working," McCartney explained. "I did a drum track and just built on it bit by bit. I didn't have any idea what the song was going to be on top of it. I put some guitars on, put the bass on and built up the backing track. Then I thought, 'What am I going to do with the voice?' I was working with a machine where you can vary the speed of the tape recorder, so you can speed your voice up or slow it down. I sped my voice up slightly, and did the vocals through a sort of echo machine I was playing around with. It's very much like sitting down with lumps of clay: you put one down and then put another down and it starts to make itself into a face or something. In this case, it made itself into the song 'Coming Up.'

"We did a tour of Britain and on the last night at Glasgow we did the new single, which was 'Coming Up.' I don't normally like to do too many new numbers on a stage show, because

McCartney: 20 Years on His Own

the audience likes what they know, generally. But there was this one kid who came down to the front and was bopping away, and I thought, 'Wow, this song is going to be a hit. It's got to mean something, he's so in to it.'"

The accompanying video featured McCartney as a variety of musical characters, including the world famous "Beatle Paul."

"It was my idea to do it," he's said, "'cause we had to think of someone to play the bass and I said, 'I could do Beatle Paul,' and the director said, 'Yeah, you gotta.' And I almost chickened out in the end. But once I did it, and put on the old uniform and got my violin bass, which has actually still got the playlist from the Beatles cellotaped to it...the moment I'd done that, I'd actually broken the whole voodoo of talking about the Beatles, 'cause I'd been him again and it didn't feel bad."

McCartney II was released in mid-May of 1980 to mostly positive reviews and great sales. The publicity McCartney had received in jail, and some first rate tracks built massive momentum. The album is funkier than anything he had done before. Some listeners may reject the more far-out material on repeated playing. There are absolutely terrific songs, such as "Coming Up," "Waterfalls," "Bogey Music" and "One of These Days." Overall the fine effort shows a Paul McCartney regaining his musical focus.

The album spawned two singles, "Waterfalls"/"Check My Machine," which somehow didn't enter the American charts and reached number seven in Britain, and "Temporary Secretary"/ "Secret Friend," which didn't make the charts at all. Both "Check My Machine" and "Secret Friend" were issued on the McCartney II CD.

Of these tracks, it's "Waterfalls" that McCartney is proudest of. It symbolizes his changing views towards songwriting.

"When I got married, things changed," he said. "Everything changes in the way you look at things...and I started to realize that I liked the warmth of a family. [I] started to realize that's important, this is important, you know, warmth and being kind of blatant about your feelings and investigating them rather than hiding them. 'Waterfalls' is basically saying, 'don't go doing all the dangerous stuff, 'cause I need you,' and that it is—that's the kind of more mature thought for me than I would have been able to have done twenty years ago. 'Cause I just didn't realize that it's not all gonna be here forever. That's the kind of thing you start to realize once you pass thirty."

By year's end, these words would haunt him.

69

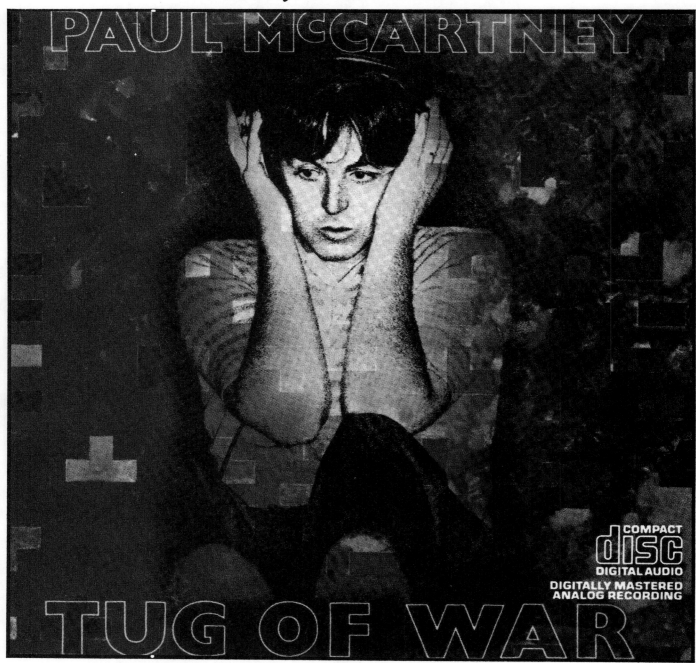

Tug of War Album Tracks: "Tug of War," "Take It Away," "Somebody Who Cares," "What's That You're Doing?," "Here Today," "Ballroom Dancing," "The Pound is Sinking," "Wanderlust," "Get It," "Be What You See," "Dress Me Up As a Robber," "Ebony and Ivory"

Tug of War was a tremendous hit in both America and Britain, topping the charts in each country

XIV. TUG OF WAR

Throughout his solo career, virtually every journalist to interview Paul McCartney invariably asked him the same question: when would the Beatles reunite? At the beginning of the Seventies, he had ruled out all possibility, responding with the cliched "it's like a divorce." As years passed, his responses gradually mellowed. After his public feuding with John Lennon ended, both reached a sort of reconciliation, neither ruling out nor encouraging reunion.

Then, when Lennon dropped out of the music scene in 1975 to spend the next five years with Yoko Ono and their son, Sean, journalists started asking what he (Lennon) was doing. McCartney tried to furnish the explanation. Then Lennon returned to the spotlight in 1980 with **Double Fantasy**, an album which, ironically, dealt with the same type of domestic issues that marked much of McCartney's solo material, which Lennon himself had previously dismissed. This led back to discussions of reunion.

"The whole Beatles reunion thing was always a non-starter, because we had all just broken up," McCartney explained for the umpteenth time. "It is like getting divorced; after you've made the big decision you don't want someone coming up and saying, 'Hey listen, I think it would be a great idea if you all got married again.' Things like money and TV exposure are not relevant. It was also the fact that we'd come full circle with the Beatles. I think we thought what we'd done was pretty special and we hadn't seen anyone else do it. I don't think [it] would ever happen. I don't think it would really be a good thing if it did. [It's all gotten] a bit legendary. It's just no use. "

Each of the Beatles echoed similar words, and they were probably right. No matter what they did, a reunion could not match the expectations the fans built up for it. Still, the *hope* was alive that the Beatles *might* get back together. *That* kept the legend alive.

The dreams of a generation died on the evening of December 8, 1980, when an assassin's bullet ended the life of John Lennon.

"Someone like John," commented McCartney, "it's like Kennedy's death. It affected *everyone*; it wasn't just Beatles lovers. I felt amazingly helpless and hopeless on the day it happened. It's not easy for me to talk about, because something like that. I don't know what my own feelings are anyway about death. I still don't know what I thought about my mom dying when I was fourteen. I know it was just a huge shock. It was similar with John, really, another huge shock and the stupidity of it all was the other terrible thing about John, and I know it was something that everybody felt. I did write a song called 'Here Today' which was kind of my reaction at the time. We had been slagging off a lot over the years. In fact, we got on quite well personally in what turned out to be towards the end. But there had been a lot of slagging off about business stuff. 'Here Today' was kind of talking to him as if he was still there. It's sort of my song remembering him, so it's kind of special to me.

"Like most people, I was kind of walking around in a daze that day. I got home that evening, put the telly (television) on and it was nothing but him. It was a very

71

emotional evening with a lot of crying. I was sort of shell-shocked. It was like, 'You're either going to sit around here all day and sit under the weight of it, or McCartney said, 'It's a drag.' That's not what I meant at all, but because I'm in the public eye, that's what happens."

Lennon's death did indeed impact on McCartney, as it helped solidify his decision to disband Wings and give up touring. Fear of a similar fate is understandable. He chose, instead, to devote his time exclusively to his music. He retired to studios in Monsterrat, where he had previously engaged in a renewed collaboration with George Martin on the album that would eventually be called **Tug of War**.

try and just keep moving and see if you could put shoes on, put one foot in front of the other and see if it would work or not,' and it did. I got to the recording studios, and George Martin was there and stuff, so that was good, because I was around somebody who had sort of known John. Back in the evening I was with my family....[Actually] I got in trouble on the day, because some newspaper guy stuck a microphone in my face and said, 'What do you think of John Lennon's death?' I knew I ought to have the perfect thing, 'John was a great friend, beloved by many people and will be missed sorely.' I knew that's what everybody's going to when that happens, and I just couldn't do it. I said, 'It's a drag,' and I meant the unholiest drags of all drags. Of course that came out in print, 'Paul

"After the Beatles," he's said, "I don't think any of us wanted to work with George. It wasn't that we didn't want to be produced by him...we all would have loved that discipline and expertise that George has....but he had been associated with the Beatles and the Beatles had broken up. We were trying to make this new career, and the press was trying to throw us back into the old career. That's why we never did Beatles songs on tours. I couldn't do them on tour for years. But once you did it, you saw how much the audience liked it. But the attraction of working with George is that I like working with him very much as a producer. He really knows what he's doing and just to be getting back with someone as professional as that, and not to be goofing off on my own, was a nice thing to do."

The first single released from these sessions was "Ebony and Ivory"/"Rainclouds," issued in March, 1982. It reached number one in America—a position it held for seven weeks—and Britain. A simple but effective plea for racial harmony, the song featured a duet between McCartney and Stevie Wonder.

"In the beginning," McCartney detailed, "I'd written this song called 'Ebony and Ivory' and it was obviously this sort of black and white racial harmony thing. I thought, 'Maybe we could do something that would suggest that kind of harmony,' so I was looking around for someone to do it with. At the time, I thought the best person in the world would be Stevie. I probably still would think that. So I got a demo to him and said, 'Here's this song I'd like to do, and I'd love you to be the other singer on it, if you'll do it.' Stevie got the message back that, yeah, he liked it and that, sure, he'd do it. I said, 'Well, we're going to Monsterrat, it would be great if we could team up there.' We got to Monsterrat, and our manager came in a bit pasty faced and said, 'We don't think Stevie's coming.' I said, 'What do you mean? He told me he's coming. He's got to come.' Luckily he was still on the phone and I said, 'Stevie, you've got to come down.' He said, 'I've got some stuff up here that I've got to do,' this elusive album **he** was always doing whenever he **didn't** want to go somewhere. But he's a lovely guy and everything, and I said, 'You've got to come up.' So I persuaded him, he came, we made the track and that was great."

On April 26th, **Tug of War** was released, and quickly reached the number one position in both the American and British charts. While **Band on the Run** is considered by many to be McCartney's masterpiece, the author believes this album holds stronger claim. As he had with negative critical reaction, sliding album and singles sales, arrest in Japan and the death of John Lennon, McCartney took adversity and channeled it into triumph. This time the re-

sult was a George Martin produced album with nary a wrong move throughout.

The album illuminates the push and pull of everyday life; of coming to grips with the past and forging ahead into the future. This theme begins in the opening title track, and runs throughout the album. No track, with the possible exception of "Ebony and Ivory," fails to add to the whole. "Ebony and Ivory" seems just a bit too light. McCartney's lyrics *mean* something, whether he's discussing highlights of his early days in "Ballroom Dancing" or his relationship with John Lennon in "Here Today." There are also the terrific collaborations with Carl Perkins on "Get It" and another Wonder title, the delightfully funky "What's That You're Doing?," as well as the wistful and sweeping "Wanderlust."

Subsequent singles released from the album were "Take It Away"/"I'll Give You a Ring" (number ten in America, number fourteen in Britain) and "Tug of War"/"Get It" (number fifty five in America, while not hitting the chart in Britain).

"Before we'd started anything, I had the title **Tug of War**," McCartney explained. "I wanted to do the whole album around that theme. The idea of conflict—that everything is a tug of war. Once or twice people did hit me with things that my music was soft or shallow. They'd ask whether I ever got fed up with writing a bit flippantly, and I said, 'Yeah, sure.' You know, I could sit down there and literally come back in three hours' time with about a hundred of those songs—and the terrifying thing is that ten of them might be big hits. I had reached a point where I thought, 'if there is some danger of being shallow, let's not—let's get more passion in it.' So **Tug of War** appealed to me."

If you were to pick up only one Paul McCartney album, this would be the one. This is his best, providing proof of how he has lasted for so long in such a changing business.

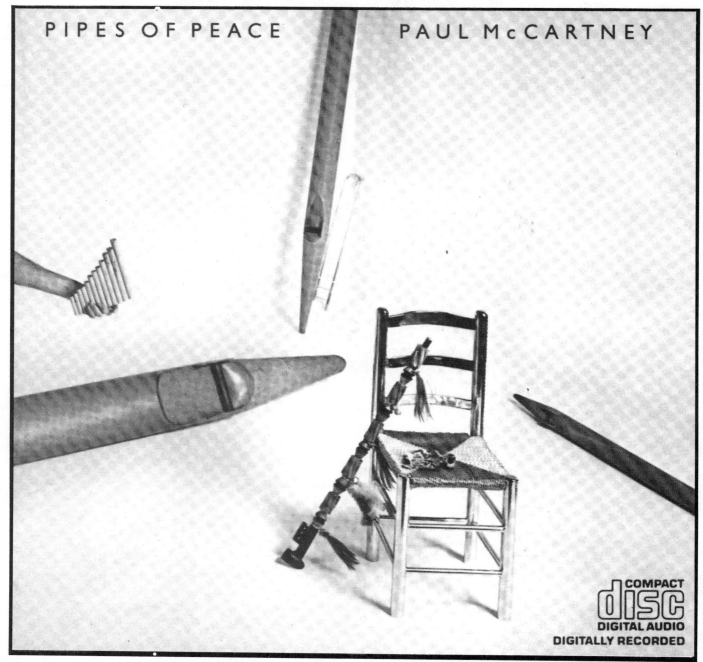

Pipes of Peace Album Tracks: "Pipes of Peace," "Say, Say, Say," "The Other Me," "Keep Under Cover," "So Bad," "The Man," "Sweetest Little Show," "Average Person," "Hey Hey," "Tug of Peace" and "Through Our Love"

XV. PIPES OF PEACE

The death
of John Lennon
caused McCartney to reflect
on his musical legacy as a Beatle and
solo artist. In that reflection he found the
strengths and weaknesses of his career, and recalled
what it had all been about in the first place: the music.

The result was the superb **Tug of War**, which demonstrated a startling maturing of songwriting prowess. Beyond that, his collaborations with Stevie Wonder proved there was nothing wrong in writing songs with other giants of the industry, even if they weren't John Lennon.

The next collaboration, with Michael Jackson, resulted in "The Girl is Mine," on of Jackson's *Thriller* album. A silly, silly love song, it reached number two in America and number four in Britain.

"Michael rang me up late back in the 1970s and I said, 'What do you want?' He said, 'I want to make some hits!' I said, 'Great, come on over.' He did and he was keen to do stuff, so I wrote 'Girlfriend' for him, which I did later on **London Town**. [Years later] we sat around upstairs on the top floor of our office in London and I just grabbed a guitar and 'Say, Say, Say' came out of it. He helped with a lot of the words on that, actually. It's not a very wordy song, but it was good fun working with him, because he's enthusiastic. But, again, it's nothing like working with John. At that stage you weren't even talking about a writer, more just a vocalist, and dancer. [Then] we wrote 'The Man' together, and then he wrote 'The Girl is Mine.' "

This collaboration ended with those three tracks, however, when Jackson eventually purchased the Beatles song catalog. "He always used to keep coming up and he'd say, 'Paul, I need some advice,' " McCartney noted to one reporter. "I'd give him that advice and say, 'Look, get good financial people, people you can trust.' I took him under my wing and we'd always be in little corridors discussing this stuff. I thought it was just fine, but he used to do this little joke. He'd say, 'I'm gonna buy your publishing, ya know.' I'd go, 'Ha! Good one, kid!' Then one day I get phoned up and they said, 'He's just bought your stuff!' I thought, 'Oh, you *are* kidding.' Anyway, Michael's got it, and all's fair in love, war and business...I suppose."

"Say, Say, Say"/"Ode to a Koala Bear" was released in October of 1983, and became a tremendous hit in both America and Britain. Unfortunately, it was McCartney's last number one hit in America.

Pipes of Peace arrived in record stores, obviously intended as a continuation of its predecessor. McCartney explained those two efforts took longer to record than any of his previous albums.

"I was working with George Martin at the AIR London and Monsterrat studios," he said. "We took a *lot* of time on those two albums. In fact, we took so much time, when I saw the bill for it all, I thought, 'I could have made an entire studio for this!' And that's in fact why I've since made my own new studio. As for the songs on those two albums, I favor the title tracks. 'Pipes of Peace' has a solid mood to it, an undercurrent that grabs you, and 'Tug of War' worked as a commentary on my career thus far; an accurate summing up.

"The whole idea of [**Tug of War**] was about a struggle of opposites, and so then instead of making **Tug of War Part II**, I decided that it was a better idea anyway to take a song I had called 'Pipes of Peace' and try and get some kind of answer in my own mind to that 'tug of war' question. In this one, the answer's obvious. It's sort of all just love."

Pipes of Peace, which peaked at number fifteen on the charts, worked quite well, but indicated a noticeable drop in lyrical quality from its immediate predecessor. As McCartney himself said, it comes to terms with the conflicts in **Tug of War**, and explains that all you need is love. The terrific title track offers pipes of peace as an answer to all the tugs of war we experience in our daily lives. The lyrics are wonderful, as is the arrangement.

Other album highlights include "Say, Say, Say", which deserved every bit of its success, a wonderful teaming of these two industry giants, as is "The Man"; "The Other Me" and "So Bad" are fine tracks in the silly love songs tradition; and there's no denying the effectiveness of "Sweetest Little Show" and "Average Person," which don't really mean very much, but make for pleasant listening. Finally, there's "Tug of Peace," which truly encapsulates the themes of both albums.

The next single from the album was "So Bad"/"Pipes of Peace" (reversed in Britain), which failed to crack the top ten.

Overall, **Pipes of Peace** continued the cyclic nature of McCartney's music: a tremendous hit album, followed by a gradual decline before a regrouping. This time the climb back up would be tougher than ever before.

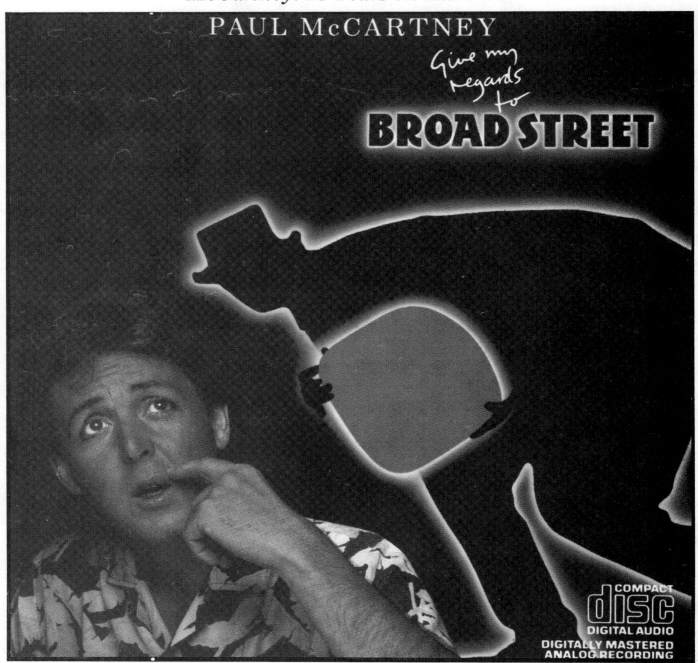

Give My Regards to Broad Street Album Tracks: "No More Lonely Nights" (ballad), "Good Day Sunshine," "Corridor Music," "Yesterday," "Here, There and Everywhere," "Wanderlust," "Ballroom Dancing," "Silly Love Songs," "Not Such a Bad Boy," "So Bad," "No Values," "No More Lonely Nights" (ballad reprise), "For No One," "Eleanor Rigby/Eleanor's Dream," "The Long and Winding Road," "No More Lonely Nights" (playout version), "Goodnight Lonely Princess"

XVI. GIVE MY REGARDS TO BROAD STREET

Beatles fans remember A Hard Day's Night and Help as a pair of wonderful films from the Sixties that capture the very essence of the Beatles when they were still the moptop Fab Four. In recent years, the majority of the band members have dismissed the films, although Paul McCartney remains the one hold-out. He explained them as a lark, and noted that he wanted to get back in front of the cameras.

Throughout the 1970s, two film ideas, the first being an adaptation of Band on the Run, turning the lyrics of the various tracks into a screenplay; the second a potential collaboration between McCartney and Star Trek creator Gene Roddenberry, which would have been a science fiction rock musical, made the rounds. The science fiction project died when Roddenberry was given the opportunity to resurrect Star Trek.

McCartney finally got his wish with Give My Regards to Broad Street, a humorous (and fictional) day in the life of the ex-Beatle as he searches for the missing tapes of his new album. The film squeezes in quite a few songs, including remakes of Beatles classics. Ringo Starr was also featured in the cast.

"The very original thing was that we were just going to play a bunch of songs for a TV show, but it grew and little bits started getting added here and there," McCartney's said. "We started to say, 'Maybe it isn't a TV show. Maybe we should add a bit of a story.' Then I actually got carried away with myself as a writer; it's a very tempting thing with these great dreams. I had a lot of time in the car going up to London a lot, so I took a pad of paper and started writing. Then we made the fatal mistake: if it's going to be an hour's TV, well a film's only an hour and a half, wouldn't be hard to extend it. But a film is a whole other beast. I saw Spielberg say recently, 'Thank God for the fifth draft.' They look at it at least five times until they think it's perfect. I just got intoxicated with the idea that I'd written it. I started telling people how to write...should have waited till it was a success.

"I think I was expecting a big team from [distributor] 20th Century Fox to come down and show me how to make the film. They leave you to get on with it. They don't interfere at all. A lot of them don't even know, [but] someone really should have said to us, 'No, this script isn't good enough. It needs fixing there, that scene's got to be there.' It wasn't that great, but it wasn't the world's greatest disaster. I think the nice thing in it is that there were some nice musical moments. I was talking to George Harrison, who was producing Shanghai Surprise, and I said, 'How's it going, George?' And he said, 'It makes Broad Street look like an epic.'"

The film bombed, taking in a paltry half a million dollars on its opening weekend, and going down from there. It did, however, inspire a top ten hit entitled "No More Lonely Nights."

"The film had to have a song from it," McCartney wryly noted. "When you've got that kind of project, it's nice to have a hit, because it all centers the attention and people say, 'If there's one hit, maybe there's two.' It makes the show look good. I like that song, but the song's a hit and the film's a flop. Some you win, some you lose and that's what you've got to consider."

While the album also featured such re-recorded tracks as "Yesterday," "Here, There and Everywhere," "Eleanor Rigby," "Ballroom Dancing" (featuring a different final verse than the version that appeared on Tug of War) and "The Long and Winding Road," it also included the brand new "Not Such a Bad Boy" and "No Values," a pair of tracks that proved McCartney could still rock with the best of them.

"I've always loved rocking," McCartney told the press. "What tends to happen is you get stuck in your own mold. Like, I read something about [Sylvester Stallone]. He's Rocky forever, that guy. You know, he tried to be a trade union leader [in F.I.S.T.] or whatever, and nobody wants him as that. So I tend to get stuck with ballads, 'cause I'm best known for that. But in actual fact, anyone who really knows the Beatles music will know there's quite a few like 'I'm Down' and 'Helter Skelter' and that kind of song, which is me anyway. So I do like that kind of stuff. That 'Not Such a Bad Boy,' Ringo and Linda demanded that got in the film, 'cause they really liked that one. It was teetering for a minute there, but they said, 'It will be in. We demand it.'"

McCartney next entered the charts with two more enjoyable movie themes. The first, "We All Stand Together," from the Rupert the Bear animated featurette, preceded Give My Regards to Broad Street, and actually climbed to number one in Britain. The second, "Spies Like Us" (backed with "My Carnival," which appears on the Venus and Mars CD), cut for the John Landis film starring Chevy Chase and Dan Aykroyd, peaked at number seven.

Number one hits were eluding McCartney in America, and sales on his albums were down. But his quest for a direction by which to address the changing music audience continued

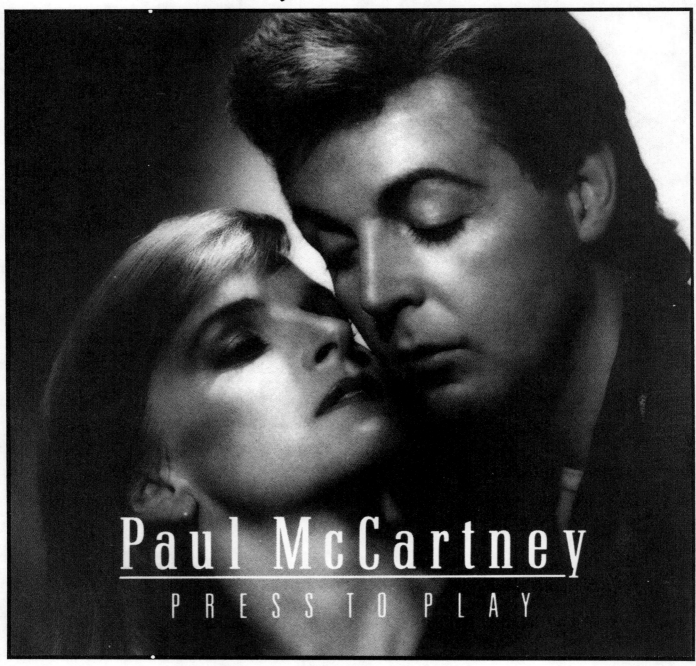

Press to Play Album Tracks: "Stranglehold," "Good Times Coming/Feel the Sun," "Talk More Talk," "Footprints," "Only Love Remains," "Press," "Pretty Little Head," "Move Over Busker," "Angry," "However Absurd," "Write Away," "It's Not True," "Tough on a Tightrope"

XVII. PRESS TO PLAY

McCartney squeezed in a pair of live performances between albums, first at the Prince's Trust Concert and then at Bob Geldorf's enormously successful Live-Aid concert, performing "Let It Be." Despite microphone problems, and part of the song being broadcast without sound, the Live-Aid put the thought of touring back in his mind. Still, as always, he didn't want to ride on the coattails of the Beatles and, now, Wings. Determined to produce an album as the basis for a world tour, his first effort was Press to Play, co-produced by Hugh Padgham.

He collaborated with Eric Stewart, from 10CC, on six of the tracks. McCartney's noted, "I'd known Eric socially when he was in the Mindbenders. He, Linda and I started doing harmonies on Tug of War and Pipes of Peace. It started very casually with Eric. I just said, 'Fancy coming round one day to try out some stuff? We started off with 'Stranglehold,' putting rhythmic words in, using lyrics like a bongo, accenting the words. We enjoyed the experience, then went on to write the six that are on the album. I remembered the old way I'd written with John, the two acoustic guitars facing each other, like a mirror, but better! Like an objective mirror. You're looking at the person playing chords, but it's not you. I'd never really tried to do that again: I'd either sit on my own with a guitar or piano or with Michael Jackson doing lyrics, or Stevie, and I just made that other one up. But it was never across the acoustics, which I'd always found a very complete way of writing."

The collaboration actually worked fairly well, as Press to Play, despite being one of his lowest selling albums ever, sounds a bit harder edged than he was known for. McCartney experimented in terms of sound, with stand-out tracks including the whimsical but nonetheless enjoyable "Press," rockers like "Talk More Talk" and "Move Over Busker" and the beautiful ballad "Footprints."

"Press" was the first single released from the album, backed with "It's Not True," which was featured on the CD release. The track did not score well in the charts.

Singles from the album, none of which broke the top ten, include "Press"/"It's Not True," "Stranglehold"/"Angry" (remix) and "Only Love Remains"/"Tough on a Tightrope." "It's Not True" and "Tough on a Tightrope" appeared on the CD release of the album.

At the time of the album's release, McCartney commented on most of the tracks in a Capital press kit as follows:

GOOD TIMES COMING/FEEL THE SUN: "There's a nostalgic air about summers that have gone. It's a pretty strong feeling, even for people who are only seventeen, they can remember a summer when they were ten. In Britain, you tend not to get too much of that stuff, so you tend to remember 'em. To me, the song is three summers: one when I was a kid going to Butlin's in my short trousers, feeling embarrassed cos I wanted long trousers. That was a good one, sort of donkeys on the beach summer. Then the second verse is a bit more grown up, when I imagine you're working, so I associate that second verse with the Beatles—'It was a silly season, was it the best? We didn't need a reason, just a rest!' That's one of my favourite lines on the album. It reminded me of the Beatles, some photos taken by Dezo Hoffman, great shots in old-fashioned Victorian bathing gear. John doing the Charleston, classic stuff. Then the third verse is kinda ominous, talking about a great summer before the war; that takes the good time edge off it. I remember I heard there were a couple of really cracking summers in 1936 and 1937, or whenever, but Hitler was just round the corner. I always imagined people playing a great game of cricket, in their whites, everything as it should be, gentle applause, tea...and then the next year they're all gonna be off at war. That's the twist in the tail of the song."

TALK MORE TALK: "The basic track was done in a day. Lyrically it was picking out quotes that I liked from, I think, a Tom Waits interview: 'I don't actually like sitting down music,' great things like that, random cut-outs. 'A master can highlight the phrases his words to digress.' I liked the surrealism of that. I like 'art' films, Bunuel, Bergman, The Seventh Seal. I could never make out what the hell they were about, but there was something attractive about the abstractness of them. So I've gone that way on 'Talk More Talk' and 'However Absurd,' which are the two main surrealist lyrics."

FOOTPRINTS: "From summer to winter. It was written on a snowy day. It came from an image of a magpie looking for food out in the snow. Eric and I changed the magpie to an old man, although the magpie came back for the third verse. The old man is out there looking for Yule logs or something, like the character in Good King Wenceslas. He's lonely. Does he live on his own? What do we know about him? The song goes into what his story might have been, the heartaches there might have been, the girl he might have left behind, the paths he didn't take, the moves he didn't make."

ONLY LOVE REMAINS: "People ask if I feel an album's incomplete without a ballad, and I do think that a little bit. I know there are people who like them who will inevitably gravitate towards that track. People who've heard the album say, 'That's the McCartney I like.' So I sorta put it on for them, and for myself, because I'm pretty romantic by nature. It's not so much the feeling, 'Now we must do the compulsory ballad,' it's more that I can write them, and I like them. I like the quiet moment, and this song is that reflective moment—and it comes at the end of side one, so if you're not in that mood, you can always take it off!"

PRESS: "Oklahoma was never like this.' That can mean whatever you want it to mean. To me, when you're writing songs, you often get a line you assume you're going to edit later, you're going to knock it out and put something sensible in. But every time I came to that line, I couldn't sing anything but, just the scanning, the way it sang. People would have understood if it it was 'Liverpool was never like this,' but it wouldn't have sung the same. It's a symbol for the provinces, the sticks, the out of the way places. The line just wouldn't change, and when you meet such resistance from the lyrics themselves, you have to give in."

PRETTY LITTLE HEAD: "That was done very quickly without thinking too much about it. I had a new studio, a new producer, a new songwriting partner, so I wanted to try something different. We'd push it a bit further just to see what would happen. That was an old philosophy of the Beatles— particularly on things like Sergeant Pepper—you'd start off with a backwards track, something zany, then you'd make up something from what it suggested. It's quite a nice way of working, a bit like abstract art. For a long while 'Pretty Little Head' was an instrumental. I drummed on it, Jerry played vibes, Eric played keyboards, so we all switched roles to send us off in a different direction. Eventually you pull it back and make some sort of sense in it. Again, the lyrics on this one are pretty exotic. I see it as a tribe who live in the hills who descend from their caves once every blue moon to bring silks and precious stones, so that their princess doesn't have to worry her pretty little head. What's kinda nice is that it can also be an ordinary family, and the pretty little head is the kid. The father protecting his family so that you won't have to worry your pretty little head."

MOVE OVER BUSKER: "That's got a good American rock 'n' roll feel to it. I think originally it was 'Move Over Buster,' which we thought was a bit ordinary, so we just kicked it a little bit and it came out 'busker,' then that gave us more possibilities about wandering round and meeting people. There's a bit of harmless sexism in it, that strong British tradition, you know, of seaside postcards. Nell Gwynne, well you know the archetypal image of her, with her oranges and all! Then there's Mae West 'in her sweaty vest'—that's an old Beatle joke 'and here's Miranda in her little sweaty vest,' just one of those insanities. Then we get Errol Flynn, looking out of his motor home, another one who was supposedly renowned for his sexual prowess."

ANGRY: "That's me being pretty straightforward, although there is a crazy synth thing on there. The back track is me, Phil Collins and Pete Townshend, which is a nice little rhythm section! That took maybe two hours, while the actual take was around 20 minutes. They're just so good those guys—you just tell Phil, 'It's a fast one and it stops here!.' What makes me angry are things like Thatcher's attitude to the blacks in South Africa and Reagan calling it South America. People who burn children with cigarettes. That sort of thing makes me angry—not bad reviews of my albums."

HOWEVER ABSURD: "It did suggest the epic finale—which is why it's at the end of the album! For me, it was another thing you start off and think 'Ooh no, that's too Beatley, so I won't do it.' So I resisted it for a little while, but I kept coming back to 'Why?' Tell me one good reason why you're resisting this Beatles influence.' Cos if anyone's got a right to do it, there's three guys alive who've got the right to do it. I've got past the point of comparisons to the Beatles, or being accused of being a 'Beatle Stylist,' but I mean, I was involved in all that stuff very heavily, and realizing it was a good system then, why ignore it now? There's a sort of

'Walrus' intro to this track, but of course any time you play that style of piano it evokes that. It's a style I know and love. The lyrics on this one are a bit bizarre, but then again they make a kind of sense, a strange kind of sense. But then I find that things in life don't always make sense, they're not always conveniently wrapped up with a little sticker that says, 'This is very sensible!' Sometimes they are completely absurd, which is what the song is about. In the middle it explains itself a bit, less surrealist: 'Something special between us....Words wouldn't get my feelings through....However absurd it may seem.' That's taking off into 'The Prophet' by Kahlil Gibran—there's a line of his that always used to attract me and John, which was 'Half of what I say is meaningless, but I say it just to reach you.' So it's that kind of meaning to 'However Absurd.'"

Press to Play released to poor reviews and sales, but as always, McCartney chose to go forward. "I do things step by step," he said. "I'm looking at getting a band together, but the difficult thing is the chemistry. A supergroup suffers from that. I prefer to go the other way and use unknown musicians. I know the Beatles used to say, 'We won't be rock and rollin' when we're forty,' but I still love it. The Prince's Trust benefit just zonked me out. It really felt great. I could do that every night. So I'd like to get a band. I don't know if I'll call it Wings. Maybe some new incarnation."

All the Best Album Tracks: "Band on the Run," "Jet", "Ebony and Ivory," "Listen to What the Man Said," "No More Lonely Nights," "Silly Love Songs," "Let 'Em In," "Say Say Say," "Live and Let Die," "Another Day," "C Moon," "Junior's Farm," "Uncle Albert/Admiral Halsey," "Coming Up," "Goodnight Tonight," "With a Little Luck," "My Love," "Once Upon a Long Ago"*
* This track was included on the disc released outside of the United States

XVIII. ALL THE BEST

Released in 1987, this second McCartney "best of" collection was marred by ten out of the seventeen (eighteen in England) tracks having already been featured on 1978's **Wings Greatest**. The reason for their inclusion a second time is difficult to discern. Even more baffling is the motive behind deleting "Once Upon a Long Ago," a charming, wistful and lovely ode to childhood, from the American release. The tracks not available on the earlier album are nice, but this remains a disappointing package.

In England, "Once Upon a Long Ago" saw release as a single, backed with "Back on My Feet," a song which marked the first collaboration between McCartney and Elvis Costello.

"The English market, or so they tell me anyway, likes compilation things and 'Hits' albums; they're very popular," McCartney said. "Whereas in the States, even if it's something like Springsteen's live compilation, apparently they reckon the market isn't as keen on stuff like that. So over here people put your hits together and then put a new song on it for a bit of interest and added enjoyment. In America, the record company was more concerned with just having the hits. I like the extra song, 'Once Upon a Long Ago,' but America for some reason didn't want it. Who am I to argue?"

In terms of "Back on My Feet" he noted, "[Elvis and I] originally said, 'Well, look, let's not *tell* anyone we're working together, because if it doesn't work, we're gonna look like idiots.' You do that, you get excited about a collaboration and then nothing really comes of it. But we've now written quite a number of songs together, and this was the first."

An interesting rocker, "Back on My Feet" showed that McCartney had found the right composing partner, a point later reinforced on **Flowers in the Dirt**.

"If someone had told me when I was a kid that, when I grew up, the land would have poisons in and the sky a hole in it, I wouldn't have believed them."

—Paul McCartney, singer, songwriter, environmental supporter

Choba B CCCP Album Tracks: "Kansas City," "Twenty Flight Rock," "Lawdy Miss Clawdy," "Bring It On Home To Me," "Lucille," "Don't Get Around Much Anymore," "That's Alright Mama," "Ain't That A Shame," "Crackin' Up," "Just Because," "Midnight Special," "I'm Gonna Be a Wheel Someday," "I'm in Love Again"

CHOBA B CCCP XIX.

In the Sixties, Beatlemania swept the globe,
touching the world in a way no band of musicians ever had
before. One primary exception, however, was the Soviet Union,
which had banned rock and roll. Through the black market some Russians
heard the music that captured the world, but in the era of glasnost, Paul McCartney
wanted to offer his friendship to Soviet fans.

This "token" of affection began in the summer of 1987 while he whipped a new band into shape for his upcoming album, and in the process recorded a variety of rock and roll classics.

"It can take a long time [to record] with computers and effects," he complained. "One day I got fed up with it and I had been jamming with some lads, some musicians, and so we decided to see if we could record like the old days—one take, two takes maximum. We ended up doing eighteen tracks in a day, which was amazing, cause it's unheard of these days. It was great and it was the nearest I'd gone in many years to getting the old sound. It's rough and ready and nobody spends hours putting equalization on the mics and setting up the computer and the drum machine. The drummers just drum it, you know. You look at the guitarist and he plays a solo."

Eventually McCartney decided to issue this album, to be titled **Choba B CCCP (Back in U.S.S.R.)**, only in the Soviet Union. As he noted, "We did those eighteen tracks and from them we have selected an album of rock and roll stuff. And it's stuff like 'Lawdy Miss Clawdy,' 'Bring It On Home to Me,' 'Kansas City'...just some weird tracks I remember from when I was about eighteen. It's going to be released, first of all, exclusively in Russia. It's kind of like a friendship thing with Glasnost and stuff. I was chuffed the way Reagan and Gorbachev were getting it on and actually becoming friendly and cutting arms. They're not cutting that many, but it's something. I thought it would be a perfect thing to do with these rock and roll tracks, to release them exclusively in Russia, just to say that you're not the backwoods anymore, you're going to get it first this time. I think [this] is kinda a special moment, 'cause when I grew up, the Iron Curtain was always there and it was Kruschev and all of them. It was always the Cold War and all that, so I think it's really great to see it loosening up a bit. I don't really know if it will be a success, but if it is, then maybe people over here will want to have a listen to it."

The man has a talent for understatement; it would be difficult to find another album so widely bootlegged as **Choba B CCCP**, and for good reason. The album is terrific, literally returning McCartney to his roots, and paving the way for his next album.

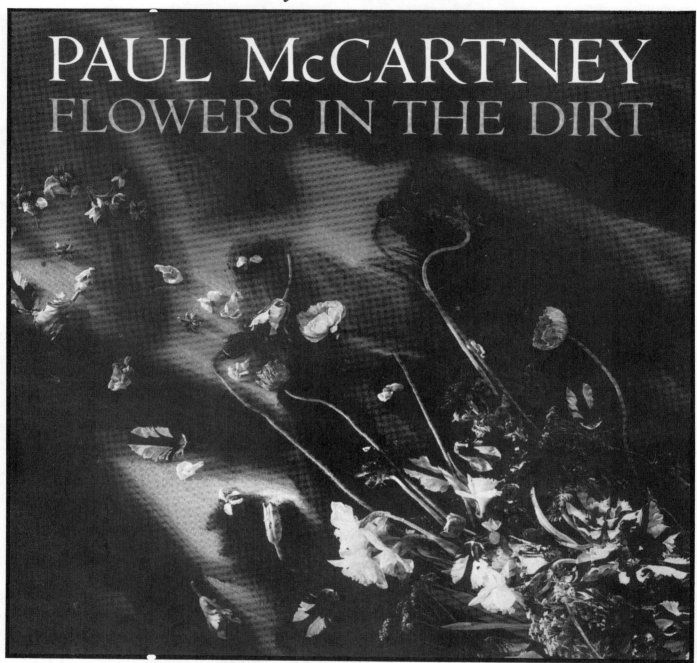

Flowers in the Dirt Album Tracks: "My Brave Face," "Rough Ride," "You Want Her Too," "Distractions," "We Got Married," "Put It There," "Figure of Eight," "This One," "Don't Be Care-less Love," "That Day is Done," "How Many People," "Motor of Love" and "Ou Est Le Soleil"

XX. FLOWERS IN THE DIRT

"I think some of the spontaneity of the Russian album carried over onto my new album," McCartney noted about his **Flowers in the Dirt**. "The longer we took on songs, the more time there was to worry and to doubt. Doing it the other way—the old fashioned way, because you didn't have forty eight tracks or whatever— you had to make decisions as you went along. It's Jerry Lee Lewis doing 'Whole Lotta Shakin.' I didn't think 'Get Back' was any kind of a single, it was a ham, and the other guys had to say, 'No, it's a great single, man.' I like that when things creep up on me. I'm not a great analyser. I'm a doer.

"I really wanted to show that I can still do it and not just rely on all the old hits," he added. "We're going out on a world tour later in the year, so it was incredibly important that I had some strong new material that was contemporary."

If that was his wish, then that's what he got. **Flowers in the Dirt** is easily his best album since 1982's **Tug of War**, falling somewhere between that disc and its follow-up, **Pipes of Peace**. While far from a masterpiece, it moves in the right direction, with fabulous lyrics and melodies. He is helped immeasurably by his backing band and the various producers, including Trevor Horn (of Frankie Goes to Hollywood fame) and Neil Dorfman. In addition, he gets tremendous aid from Elvis Costello, who collaborates on four tracks (two additional numbers are featured on Costello's *Spike*).

"He's a very good foil for me," said McCartney, "and I think we foil each other fine. I was looking for a collaborator, I asked around and somebody suggested Elvis Costello. I liked the stuff of his I'd heard, so he came down here, and we had some fun finishing a couple of songs he'd started. Then we sat down and said, 'Let's write something from scratch.' That's when the fun really started! Like, where do we start? So I think I suggested Smokey Robinson and the Miracles, a nice starting point for anyone. So we wrote a sort of soul-y thing, that needless to say turned out nothing like Smokey and the Miracles! That was called 'Lovers That Never Were.' It isn't on the album—it's good though. We continued 'till we'd written nine songs together, and then whittled those down to the four on the album.

"It seemed to me with Elvis that he was very good, but occasionally he started to ramble, he's very wordy. I once said to him, 'Have you got any ideas?' I had to laugh. 'Have I got any ideas?' He pulled out three bags, about fifty books full of ideas! He jots down anything he overhears in those books. I must say that working with Elvis reminded me of working with John. We did have some laughs/coming to blows/differences of opinion. I'd say, 'Put a bit of echo on the drums.' He'd say, 'No! No echo.' Later I'd say, 'Maybe a bit of chorus on that guitar?' 'God, no. No chorus!' 'How about a synth thing then, El?' 'Not synthesisers?' So of course by the time he'd finished his own album, he'd used chorus, echo, synthesiser and the kitchen sink! But it was quite good fun, because we rubbed off on each other."

All four of their collaborations on **Flowers in the Dirt** sound great, from the very Beatleish "My Brave Face" to "You Want Her Too," essentially a superior and more mature version of "The Girl is Mine," as well as the ballad "Don't Be Careless Love" and "That Day is Done."

Not to imply that McCartney needs Costello to excel on this album; he handles himself just fine, thank you. "We Got Married" is the kind of audio-diary that John and Yoko used to do in the early Seventies, and it's terrific, detailing the relationship between Mr. and Mrs. McCartney; "Put It There" is a touching tribute to his father, James; "Figure of Eight" is a good rocker and "This One" is the type of combination rocker/ballad that he has always excelled at.

As with **Press to Play**, McCartney took the time to go over each track with Capital's P.R. department, and the results are as follows:

MY BRAVE FACE: "Well...the first single off the album is...'My Brave Face,' which me and Elvis wrote together. As I say, after we'd done the fixes on his and the fixes on mine, we then sat down and started writing songs from the ground up that neither of us had any pre-conceptions about, and one of those, after we'd written quite a few, was called 'My Brave Face' and it was good. There was a nice equal kind of collaboration on it, we'd just sort of throw words about and stuff and where I thought he was getting maybe a bit too cryptic or whatever, I'd just say, 'I don't like that, we should go a bit further here, or we should maybe take it there' and it was nice. If he spotted an idea he liked, then we'd go that way or similarly with me. So that was quite good. But as I say, we got around to 'My Brave Face' and it's got a kind of Sixties-ish feel."

ROUGH RIDE: "I was going to work with Trevor Horn and Steve Lipson, and I'd heard—well everyone had heard—that Trevor takes a long time. I really didn't want to take too long, so it seemed to me that it might be a good idea if we could try and limit him to a short period and see what we could get done. Just see if we liked each other, because, you know, with an album you don't want to commit yourself and then have to cancel the whole thing because you don't get on. So I asked my manager to ask them if they'd be interested in seeing if we could finish a whole track

over two days. I played Trevor a lot of song-y songs, songs that were finished and ready to go. He didn't seem that interested, and I felt like I was bloody auditioning. Then he said, 'Have you got anything else?' I said, 'Well, I've got this crazy little thing you won't like, it's called "Rough Ride."' He said, 'I love the title already.' I played it, and it was like a 12-bar, me trying to be Big Bill Broonzy! I'd seen a blues program and I thought, 'Well, these guys do a song and it's all one chord, two verses and a little guitar riff [singing] 'Chung-a-Chung: Wanna rough ride; chung-a-chung: to Heaven, oh yeah...' ' That's all I had, and it grew from a nothing, little 12-bar and by the end of the second day we'd mixed it, which is pretty unheard of these days. In fact, they remixed it and then came back assuming like everyone does these days that it can't be finished in two days, so they came back with a tarted up version, and I said, 'Well, I think it's a Paul Goes to Hollywood, Frankie Goes to McCartney type of thing,' so we kept the original."

YOU WANT HER TOO: "I said to Elvis, 'Look, this is really getting a bit me and John, I'm being Paul and you're really being John!' I'm going 'I've loved her so long' and he's saying, 'I know you did, you stupid git!' I said, 'My God, that's me and John's whole style, I'd write some romantic line and John does some sort of acid acerbic put down.' Elvis agreed it was a bit like that, so I did a version answering myself, as my conscience, but it didn't sound right, really corny, so we reinstated his version, works much better. The intro and the fade we decided to have a little strange carousel thing we'd worked up. It was a silly little idea of mine that I think works, a sort of strange little fairground. I'd had this idea about a little guitar thing that Hamish [Stuart] had played in the instrumental bit; I'd always been hearing it like a big brass band. So we actually got a big band in one morning, and it's the ultimate tease, because they play, and as soon as you're into them—they fade!"

DISTRACTIONS: "And then there's

another song I wrote called 'Distractions,' which is fairly 'oobli.' There's a nice story about that. I heard an album a few years ago by someone off Prince's lave, Paisley Park, called the Family. I don't know if you ever heard that, it was just a husband and wife, I think. And it was quite a good record. And there were some string arrangements on it that were really interesting and I listened to the record and I thought, 'Wow, great, I wonder who this is?,' so I looked on the cassette and it said Clare Fischer. I thought, 'Wow,' you know, 'this is amazing, it's probably some sort of L.A. girl and she's like long hair and does these amazing arrangements, and probably like a great classical...,' and I started to build up this pedestal figure of this amazing person. So I said to Linda, 'These arrangements are incredible and it's this Clare Fischer, you know, some L.A. chick, I think,' and she said, 'I'm not that keen on these arrangements, they're not that good,' and while she thought it was this great blonde L.A. lady, she didn't like them. We found out, actually, it's this guy who's about fifty years old, who's got a grey beard and he's a great fellow, but it's not at all this gorgeous L.A. chick, it's a man called Clare Fischer. And he's brilliant. So the next minute Linda was saying, 'I love these arrangements, I love this guy's work.' That's wives, you know. Anyway, with this track 'Distractions,' he did an arrangement for it which I love. It's very Hollywood and the nearest time frame I could associate it with is Doris Day movies, which is a very strange little area, you know, but it's lovely. And there was a funny thing on the session: Clare Fischer was conducting and he said, 'Excuse me, could you play it exactly like the first violin here?' He said, 'He's playing it exactly right.' So all the other musicians went, 'Oh dear, he's right...' and the guy, he's kind of a New York type guy, moved to Hollywood, he takes his fingers and he's holding the violin and he kisses his fingers and he goes 'I love you, you little money-makers!' Which I thought was great and it was a nice, fun session. And the music's the main thing: I really

like the arrangement he did. It just does something for me."

WE GOT MARRIED: "It's like a celebration of marriage. It's also one of the first things we tried in this new studio. So often people shy away from subjects like marriage, they go to 'when we meet baby, I'll carry your books home from school.' They concentrate on puberty. Well, at the age of 46, puberty's fairly far away! The game is up, folks, on the puberty bit. So I got more interested in looking at my situation, which is marriage and a lot of people I know are married, and very happy with it, and it's not a shameful subject at all. I do actually start it in puberty: 'Going fast, coming soon/We made love in the afternoon/ Found a flat, after that/ We got married.' That reminds me of John and Cynthia at Art School. Then it goes through time, and the last verse talks about everything going by very fast, which is a phenomenon for me at this point—things seem to fly by at the speed of light. David Gilmour's on there playing lovely guitar. I like it. It's kinda grown up."

PUT IT THERE: "'Put It There'...is an expression my dad used to say when we were kids. He used to hold out his hand and say, 'Put it there if it weighs a ton.' And, you know, you remember those things. My dad died over ten years ago, but you remember those things with affection. And so I wrote a song about that, which I like, which I think will become one of my favorites."

FIGURE OF EIGHT: "Very spontaneous, very rough, another two day effort with Trevor. Having done 'Rough Ride,' I said, 'Well, I love this. I think this is great limiting you to two days.' We had to do things quickly and decide things quickly, which was a good discipline for all of us. The vocal is live, which I like, with all the roughness. People say, 'Well, you ought to fix it.' To me, that's what's interesting about now and this album—working with people who are used to being very finished and accurate. I'm not really a great admirer of that, so what I'm trying to do is force them to come a little bit towards what I like, which is loose ends and roughness."

THIS ONE: "The song is basically a love song—did I ever say I love you? And if I didn't, it's because I was waiting for a better moment, and one hasn't come along, so here you go: I love you! But then, 'There never could be a better moment than this one...,' and the words 'this one' kept coming to me as 'this swan,' and I got off on that. 'The swan is gliding above the ocean/A God is riding on his back/How calm the water and bright the rainbow? Fade this one to black.' The image, then, once I had this swan, was like one of those Hare Krishna posters that I used to see a lot in India. You have this idyllic picture and this little blue God with flowers all over him, and that's Krishna, who's riding on this swan floating over this beautifully clear pond with lovely pink lillies on it. It's a very spiritual, tranquil picture, and on the nice moments from a lot of them. It's a peaceful, idyllic image for me, so I say, 'There could never be a better moment than this one.'"

THAT DAY IS DONE: "We did a series of sessions, Elvis and me co-producing. Got a great feel on them, a nice little live vibe, a lot of spirit, but a little bit unfinished, so we remade them, but kept certain elements and arrangements...we kept the piano and vocal and added some Hovis Brass to give it a silver band/New Orleans marching band feel. I said to Elvis, 'Look, man, we're trying to make records, scintillating fab hit records that are gonna make people go, "Wow!"' I kept bringing in all these happening hits, and Elvis was bringing in like Eskimo drum music and the Bulgarian All Stars! On 'That Day is Done' I said, 'Oh yeah, I get it. New Orleans funeral music. House is finished, right?' It's turned out a nice track set against everything else on the album."

HOW MANY PEOPLE?: "Me in Jamaica on holiday. It's reggae. In Jamaica you can't help going reggae, everybody is, the climate is. I've been a reggae fan since the early *Tighten Up* albums; ska and bluebeat seemed a little bit more towards calypso, but I fell for reggae. We went to Jamaica and bought a pile of 45's, the B-sides are just crazy. I once found a record there called 'Poison Pressure' by Lennon/McCartney! And I tried to find one of our songs in that, but that's the Jamaican thing, it doesn't have anything to do with what it says on the label. My fondness goes all the way back to 'C Moon.' I was on holiday there recently, and this very simple song called 'How Many People' came out. I thought it was too simple, I ought to complicate it, then I thought that's a silly idea, so we kept it simple."

MOTOR OF LOVE: "I don't sit down to write 'A Big Ballad.' It's whatever mood I'm in. I wrote that last year. We made a version I wasn't too happy with, but I liked the song. It was gonna get dumped off the album. We'd done a lot of work on the album by this time, so I said, 'Why don't we give it to some independent people off the album, get some objectivity? I think it's a good song and it might get back as a contender.' I'd liked Chris Hughes and Ross Cullum's work with Tears For Fears, Red box and people, and they worked up a more modern, hi-tech version. It's slow, so you call it a ballad. But it could have ben speeded up like crazy and you'd have called it Punk! 'Heavenly Father' is an old trick for me, it's like 'Mother Mary.' I have a father, 'look down from above....' That's more how I thought of it when I wrote it, but I realized the moment you say 'Heavenly Father' or 'Mother Mary' there's also that connotation. I like a bit of God thought, nothing wrong with that!"

ON EST LE SOLEIL: "There's another wacko track where we decided to make something up. This is always a fatal idea, because you're off in no-no-land from the word go. It's like, 'What's the song then?' 'Well, we don't know.' 'Well, how does it go?' 'We don't know.' 'What's the title?' 'We don't know.' 'What are the chords?' 'We don't know.' 'What instrument...?' Which is generally what you don't want to be doing in the studio, but because we had this slightly

different approach we decided to do it like that. So for about four days it was another song; it had a whole other sort of set of lyrics, something about 'Valley Road'—it was a silly way to work, really. Anyway, after about four or five days we hated it and I think we were just about to go home. Well, we didn't hate it that much. We liked the backing and stuff, but we didn't like where the song was going and Trevor said, 'Have you got anything for one of the verses that we could just...have you got any ideas?' And I said, 'Well, I've got this really silly idea that I had from years ago,' which is just some French works that say 'Ou est le Soleil? Dans la tete. Travailliez.' Those are the complete lyrics. So I went out and sang that and they said, 'Love it!' So we've got this silly French dance track now, which I love! And for me, this is what I was saying before about concept. I mean, literally those are the lyrics: 'Ou est le soleil? Dans la tete. Travaillez.' Some-body heard it the other day and said, 'There's some French words in there, aren't there?'!

Flowers in the Dirt works as a co-meback vehicle for McCartney, whetting the appetites of fans. Unfortunately, sales indicate he still has some distance to go. Despite critical acclaim, the public has not shown their support at the cash register. Even the cassette and vinyl singles it's inspired, "My Brave Face"/"Flying to My Home," "This One"/"The First Stone," "Ou Est Le Soleil," backed with an instrumental version, and "Figure of Eight"/"Ou Est Le Soleil" have charted poorly.

Continued efforts like this and the **Flowers in the Dirt** world tour will provide Paul McCartney with the chance to touch a chord with the disc-buying public, allowing him the opportunity to rise from the ashes a second time, continuing an unprecedented career in music.

XXI. AND IN THE END....

On the night of December 11, 1989, Paul McCartney and his band, consisting of Chris Witten, Robbie McIntosh, Hamish Stuart, Paul "Wix" Wickens and Linda McCartney, took the stage of Madison Square Garden bringing his Flowers in the Dirt world tour to New York.

A different McCartney stood behind the microphone than the one who had played the city thirteen years earlier as the leader of Wings. The confidence was still there, to be sure, but—as he had proven on prior venues on this tour—he was a man who had come to grips with his past; who had no problems digging into his Beatles period as well as his solo years to provide the audience with one hell of a show.

And a hell of a show it was, as McCartney and company tore into a variety of songs which ran the gamut of his career, from his early rock and roll roots to Flowers in the Dirt.

After an eleven minute film tracing his career in film clips and music, culminating in the word "Now," McCartney and his band roared onto the stage performing his latest single, "Figure of Eight." The audience rocked with the sound and, for the majority of the two hour show, never stopped.

McCartney followed with "Jet," from his Wings days, garnering a tremendous response; the seemingly less anticipated "Rough Ride" off the new album and nearly brought the roof down when he broke into strains of "Got to Get You into My Life." By then the audience writhed in fits of rock 'n roll ecstasy. At that moment, McCartney returned delivering the enduring power of the Beatles. It served as final proof he had finally come to grips with his legacy.

From there McCartney segued into "Band on the Run," the lacklusterly received "Ebony and Ivory," the newly minted "We Got Married," the enduring "Maybe I'm Amazed." He then returned to business with a variety of Beatles songs, including "The Long and Winding Road" and "The Fool on the Hill," dedicated to John, George and Ringo, during which he rose twenty feet in the air on a rotating piano. Next up came "Sgt. Pepper's Lonely Hearts Club Band," followed by the song's reprise from the end of the album of the same name (both featuring incredible guitar work); "Good Day Sunshine" and "Can't Buy Me Love," which sounded remarkably like the record he and the other Fabs cut some twenty five years before, followed.

After the Beatles tunes came the new album's "Put it There," which the band capped off with a brief musical reprise taken from "Hello, Goodbye," and then it was back to Beatles territory again with "Things We Said Today" and"Eleanor Rigby."

After that McCartney returned to Flowers in the Dirt with "This One" and the superb "My Brave Face," both of which will undoubtedly be counted among his classics some day. Then, showing complete awareness of which buttons to push, he and the band—which played with barely a wrong move throughout the night—shifted back to the Beatles and the indestructible "Back in U.S.S.R." Somehow this song is more fitting than ever now. This was followed in turn by "I Saw Her Stand-

ing There".

Then he returned to his roots with "Twenty Flight Rock," shifted to the 80's with "Coming Up," a statement regarding Friends of the Earth, and took a trip back in time to "Let It Be," and yet further back to the searing "Ain't That A Shame." Returning to his solo years, "Live and Let Die," was played to the accompaniment (as many of the songs were) of a dazzling laser light display that worked in perfect synchronization and exploding pyrotechnics on stage.

The band launched into "Hey Jude," and a concluding chorus that brought all of Madison Square Garden singing along for the ride. The extremely powerful moment once again demonstrated the impact McCartney has had on two generations of music lovers.

Then it was over. Or so it seemed, until applause, cheering, hand clapping and foot stomping brought the group back on stage, where McCartney performed a solo of "Yesterday," rocked with "Get Back" and concluded the night with "Golden Slumbers/Carry That Weight," in an absolutely perfect rendition taken from the Beatles' Abbey Road.

Paul McCartney left the stage thirteen years after his last appearance, proving he had not lost his rock and roll soul and his career was far from over.

As his world tour proceeds, and he continues writing and recording, McCartney remains philosophical over the peaks and valleys of his music of the past twenty years.

"In years to come," he states in the world tour program book, "people may actually look at all of my work rather than the context of it following the Beatles. And with John's work too. They'll look at it in greater detail and think, 'Ah, I see what he was getting at.' Because it's not obvious, that's the good thing about it. It's a little bit more subtle than some of the stuff we've done, which is straight out and commercial.

"The interesting thing is that there's always young people coming up and they don't know all the legends that have gone by. In fact, it was the Liverpool lad from Smash Hits, he was telling me when George had his hit 'Got My Mind Set On You,' he said they had letters in saying, 'Who is this George Harrison guy?' That's what time does. They're little kids. They don't know. There was a time when you thought there would never come a time when people wouldn't know who George Harrison or the Beatles are. Too famous, could never fade out, and yet there it was, large as life. People asking, 'Who is he?'

"So I always found that optimistic, actually, particularly if you're trying to do something after the Beatles. You know, is there life after the Beatles? It was always good that there were young people coming up, because then you could play to them and not feel like you were just trying to outdo your own legend. Which is a piss-off. It's like if you've been an astronaut and you've been to the moon, what do you do with the rest of your life? Get religion, most of them do, and go on lecture tours saying, 'I saw God on the moon.'"

"It's hard to follow my own act," he admitted elsewhere. "But the only answer to that would be to give up after the Beatles. I only had two alternatives. Give up or carry on. And having elected to carry on, I couldn't stop."

APPENDIX

THE McCARTNEY BOOTLEGS

Reviews By Mark Wallgreen

"RAVING ON": LP, Sandwich Records SR 7980
Side 1: "Mr. H Adams," "Summer's Day Song," "Do You Know I'll Get You Baby?," "Bubbles"
Side 2: "Raining In My Heart," "It's So Easy," "Bo Didley"

This recent European release features McCarTney recordings not found on previous bootlegs. The first side contains four outtakes from the **McCartney II** sessions, two of which are vocals and two of which are instrumentals. Unfortunately, the best of the four songs, "Mr. H Adams," has the poorest sound quality of them all. An all-out high-tech rocker, this song definitely should have been included on the commercial release. Next up is an instrumental version of a song which did make the final LP, "Summer Day Song." The third track offered here is listed on the cover as "Rock Little Baby," but upon closer listening one can hear Paul actually singing the lyrics "Do You Know I'll Get You Baby?," which is how I have listed it here. It is another uptempo number, far better than a lot of the numbers included on the commercial album. Closing out the side is an experimental instrumental called "Bubbles," which sounds exactly like that! In other words, Paul fooling around and coming up with "electronic" bubble sounds.

Side two was recorded September 14, 1979 during Buddy Holly week, and two of three songs here feature Paul on lead vocals. Denny Laine sings "Raining in My Heart" to kick it off, followed by Paul taking lead vocal on "It's So Easy" and "Bo Didley." The sound quality is fairly good, coming from a video recording that circulates among collectors.

The album features a black and white cover with a photo of Paul on the front and song titles on the back. Despite the less than thrilling sound quality of the **McCartney II** material, it is nonetheless an essential item for McCartney collectors. As Paul stated in interviews at the time, he has so much left-over material that **McCartney II** could have been a double album. Hopefully more of these tracks will surface (and hopefully in better sound quality next time).

COMPLAINT TO THE QUEEN: LP, Maisie BTA-005
Side 1: "I'll Give You A Ring," "Maisie," "I Would Only Smile," "Send Me the Heart," "Ebony and Ivory," "Waterspout" and "Waterfalls"
Side 2: "Hi Hi Hi," "Arrow Through Me," "Winter Rose," "Love Awake," "Old Siam, Sir," "Weep For Love," "Complaint to the Queen" and "Eat at Home" (intro only)

A color photo close-up of Paul taken from the indoor videotaping of the "Paperback Writer" and "Rain" clips in 1966 fills the front cover of this recent McCartney bootleg from Brazil. Inside, one will find what amounts to the **Suitable For Framing** album featuring various B-sides, alternate mixes and unreleased items. Two songs from that previous LP have been deleted here (gone are "Rainclouds" and "Take It Away") and replaced with two others ("Old Siam, Sir" alternate mix from the same tape as the other material found here from **Back to the Egg**; and a partial recording of the guitar-solo introduction to "Eat At Home" from a 1972 Wings live concert in Europe). The rest of the material, as noted, comes from **Suitable For Framing**, with slight rearranging in a different running order.

The sound quality is extremely poor, even for an album reproduced from another bootleg, and the pressing is similarly bad, with an abundance of snap, crackles and pops. The LP's title is a take-off on the previous European bootleg **Complaint to the Queen**. Unless you have to own simply "everything," this one will be easy to pass up.

COLD CUTS: LP, Club Sandwich Records SP-11
Side 1: "A Love For You," "My Carnival," "Waterspout," "Momma's Little Girl," "Night Out" and "Robber's Ball"
Side 2: "Cage," "Did We Meet Somewhere Before?," "Hey Diddle," "Tragedy," "Best Friend" and "Same Time Next Year"

In the tradition of such legendary bootlegs as **Get Back, Somewhere in England, The Beatles at the Hollywood Bowl** and **Sessions,** comes yet another completed but otherwise unreleased Fab-related LP sure to excite McCartney fans everywhere: the oft talked about **Cold Cuts** album of unreleased songs which Paul has been toying with since as far back as 1974. The twelve-track line-up was put together in 1980 for intended early 1981 release, but the murder of John Lennon put the project on hold once again.

The one dozen unreleased selections represent material recorded and mixed between 1971 ("Momma's Little Girl") and 1980. There is one live recording made during 1972's Wings Over Europe tour ("Best Friend") and two songs written specifically as motion picture themes ("Did We Meet Somewhere Before?" and "Same Time Next Year"), though neither was used as intended. Only one song is a cover version, Wings' remake of the 1961 hit "Tragedy" (originally by the Fleetwoods). The other eleven songs are all McCartney compositions.

"Did We Meet Somewhere Before?" was written as the theme song for *Heaven Can Wait,* but ultimately settled for background duty in *Rock 'n Roll High School.* It is one of the stronger and more appealing ballads McCartney has recorded on his own and deserves to be released officially. "My Carnival" will be instantly recognizable, having been issued at long last in late 1985 as the B-side to "Spies Like Us." This is an entirely different edit/mix of the song which gives further clues as to how Paul went back into the studio from time to time to remix material. Live versions of "Best Friend" appeared on bootlegs previously, as several exist covering that original 1972 European tour by Wings. The final familiar track is "Waterspout"—a **London Town** outtake—which appears in a much longer version — by some two minutes!— than found on any prior bootleg.

That leaves the entirely "new" material. Among the more inspired and certainly deserving (of official release) "gems" are: "A Love For You," one of the more adventurous and catchy tunes McCartney has laid down. His oddly infectious vocal style (slightly high in pitch and somewhat strained) couples with a driving rhythm provided by acoustic guitar and drums for a winning result. This track could have easily been included on **Press to Play** (perhaps Paul's most "adventurous" album).

"Cage" is another unqualified hit, a song-within-a-song ala "Band on the Run" and "Venus and Mars-Rock Show," wherein Paul has successfully blended two different tunes. This could have been another hit single for McCartney at any time. The other movie theme, "Same Times Next Year" (meant for the film of the same title, but never used) is a more traditional McCartney piano ballad backed with heavy strings and orchestration, most notably for the odd-timing of McCartney's phrasing in places. The album's most "rocking" number would undoubtedly be "Night Out," a high-tech all-out screamer that demonstrates that Paul has never completely forgotten how to rock.

One of the most unusual songs in the McCartney catalog is "Robber's Ball," something of a mini-opera with Paul tackling a variety of voices and vocal styles. It succeeds where perhaps "More Moose and the Grey Goose" (on **London Town**) fails. "Momma's Little Girl" and "Hey Diddle" are two of the "simpler" tunes found here, dating from 1971 and 1974, respectively. Lots of acoustic guitar, harmonic vocals from Linda and a good deal of "down home" feeling persists in both tracks, though some might find them tedious as opposed to charming.

Best news of all for collectors: this incredible record is presented in very good stereo sound quality on a clean pressing. It is packaged in a color cover picturing a kiddie's record player on which a "cold cut" (piece of luncheon meat) is spinning! Released on the Club Sandwich label, **Cold Cuts** scores a definite "must" for all Beatles/McCartney fans.

EGGS UP: LP, Cage Records 01979
Side 1: "Reception," "Cage," "Getting Closer," "We're Open Tonight," "Spin it On," "Old Siam, Sir" and "Again and Again and Again"
Side 2: "To Your," "Arrow Through Me," "After the Ball," "Million Miles," "Winter Rose," "Love Awake," "The Broadcast," "Rockestra Theme" and "So Glad to See You Here"

This excellently produced European underground release virtually presents an alternate version of the 1979 **Back to the Egg** album. Consisting of complete, full-length pre-final mixes and alternate takes (not to mention at least one completely unreleased track), **Eggs Up** is a superb McCartney package which should appeal to serious collectors as well as casual fans. If you enjoy the **Back to the Egg** album, you'll definitely enjoy this. If not, you'll probably dislike this—but a few may be pleasantly surprised.

For the collector there are numerous alternate mixes and even a few outtakes. Most notable is "Cage," which appears in an entirely different take and mix than the version which already appeared on the U.S. **Cold Cuts** album. This version seems more tame. Among the most significant items: a different take of "Getting Closer" with Denny Laine sharing much of the lead vocal duties, and alternate mixes (with noticeable differences) of "To You," "Rockestra Theme" and "So Glad to See You Here." Another major difference occurs with the opening track, "Reception," which is much longer here and certainly more interesting than the brief and ineffective snatch included in the official album. The two medley numbers and the spoken word "Broadcast" are the same as in the issued mixes.

Eggs Up is packaged in a deluxe full-color laminated cover with a color photo of the 1979 Wings line-up on the front, and a series of eggs and song titles on the back (all taken from the official songbook of the LP). It's not every day that an entire alternate version of an official album release is made available on bootleg with excellent sound quality.

WAR AND PEACE: LP, Instant Analysis BBR 015
Side 1: "Ballroom Dancing," "Take It Away," "Dress Me Up as a Robber #1," "The Pound is Sinking," "Keep Under Cover #1," "Average Person," "Dress Me Up As a Robber #2" and "Sweetest Little Show"
Side 2: "Ebony and Ivory," "The Pound is Sinking #2," "Keep Under Cover #2," "Dress Me Up As a Robber #3," "Wanderlust," "Take Her Back Jack," "We All Stand Together" and "Boil Crisis"

In 1981, when McCartney began recording the project that would ultimately emerge in early '82 as **Tug of War**, he brought to those sessions far more material that would be needed when George Martin determined that a strong single-LP would be produced rather than Paul's originally intended double set. Some of the tracks first worked on during **Tug of War** eventually made their way onto the 1983 follow-up release, **Pipes of Peace**. Material from both, along with completely unreleased and never before available McCartney compositions, are presented here on the appropriately titled **War and Peace**.

Naturally, of most interest will be the two brand new songs. "Take Her Back Jack" is a mid-tempo boogie number that moves right along and certainly would have worked well on **Pipes of Peace**. The amusing lyrics deal with the singer's warnings to his friend about the uncertainty of his female companions' prior whereabouts and sexual activity. All tongue-in-cheek and all in fun. Likewise, "Boil Crisis," a song first recorded by Wings back in 1977 for the **London Town** album, reported at the time to be McCartney's first "punk-rocker" (it eventually lost that distinction to "Spin It On" on the **Back to the Egg** LP). This 1981 run-through still packs plenty of punch and features a very unique vocal combination, shifting back and forth from a screaming and screeching to spoken word delivery. The all-out humor in these lyrics far surpasses the words found in "Take Her Back Jack," with McCartney extolling the hardships of having boils on your nose, your neck, and so on. Certainly one of the more unusual but intriguing tracks which Paul has never seen fit to issue in any form to date!

Another recording of great interest is "We All Stand Together," which Paul had officially recorded in late 1980 and eventually issued worldwide (except the U.S.) in December '84 (at the same time the Rupert, the Bear cartoon featurette was issued, playing on the same bill in some theatres with the **Broad Street** movie). This 1981 recording is a live studio version which virtually duplicates the finished product—no small feat, given the ultra-high-pitched vocal and numerous background noises.

The remaining recordings are all working versions of familiar tunes which, as noted, found their way onto **Tug of War** and **Pipes of Peace**, and for the most part are pretty much similar to the final versions. Various lyrics do differ, such as in "The Pound is Sinking." This is the first set of these outtakes to appear on bootleg, so collectors will no doubt wish to add this bountiful set of rare McCartney studio recordings to their personal archives.

It should be noted that these works feature full instrumentation (guitars, bass, electric piano, drums, et al) and are by no means merely acoustic or piano solo demos. The sound quality is generally good throughout, though the sound level dips in a few places. The bootleggers have annoying fade-ins and fade-outs in each track so you lose the opening and closing notes. It would be nice if in the future such material was left intact.

First issued in a plain jacket with a paper insert cover and subsequently in a fabricated cover, **War and Peace** will not disappoint serious McCartney fans.

JAMES PAUL McCARTNEY: LP, Club Sandwich JPM 41673
Side 1: "Big Barn Red," "Blackbird," "Bluebird," "Michelle," "Heart of the Country," "Mary Had a Little Lamb," "Little Woman Love," "C-Moon," "My Love" and "Uncle Albert/Admiral Halsey"
Side 2: "Gotta Sing, Gotta Dance," "Live and Let Die," "The Mess," "Maybe I'm Amazed," "Long Tall Sally" and "Yesterday"
This recent offering from the folks at Club Sandwich Records stands as undoubtedly the premiere packaging job of Paul's ABC-TV special which aired in the U.S. on Monday evening, April 16th, 1973. In the program, McCartney served up a variety of solo (Wings) and even Beatles tunes, presented in a number of different settings and running the gamut from concert stage to Hollywood-type production to playing all alone on acoustic guitar. In all, McCartney featured no less than 16 songs (17, counting "Hi Hi Hi," which was cut from the American broadcast, but left in the British airing), and every one of those tracks is included on this album.

While soundtrack bootlegs to this special have appeared dating back to mid 1973, this is definitely the best sound-quality presentation. The packaging is without a doubt the best yet. Issued in a deluxe full-color jacket, the front features a spectacular *TV Guide* simulation with Paul pictured on the front in a shot from the special, and an amazing and quite amusing back-cover send-up of the inside of the magazine, showing listings and a Close-Up feature on the special—all of which look quite convincing (unless you happen to own an original *TV Guide* issue from that week in 1973).

This album should appeal greatly to newer or younger fans who may otherwise by unfamiliar with this show, as well as longtime followers who would just as soon replace their early paper insert jacket copies with this pressing of higher quality and value.

THE LOST McCARTNEY ALBUM-THE UNRELEASED McCARTNEY II LP, Club Sandwich Records GTF-222
  Side 1: "Front Parlour," "Frozen Jap," "All You Horseriders" and "Blue Sway"
  Side 2: "Temporary Secretary," "On the Way," "Mr. H Atom," "Summer's Day Song," "You Know I'll Get You Baby" and "Bogey Wobble"
  Side 3: "Darkroom," "One of These Days," "Secret Friend" and "Bogey Music"
  Side 4: "Check My Machine," "Waterfalls," "Nobody Knows" and "Coming Up"

This is the original two-record version of **McCartney II**, which Paul first turned in to EMI (and presumably CBS Records in America) in early 1980 to consider for release. Ultimately, the twin package was substantially pared down to a single LP for release in the late spring of that same year. Quite obviously, the record issued differed considerably from this original 18 track, 81 minute double set.

Paul recorded all of this material at his home over the summer of 1979, and toyed with the idea of issuing it throughout the remainder of the year. Following his drug bust in Japan in January, 1980 and the subsequent break-up of Wings, he saw the path clear for its release in early 1980.

As noted, the original two-record version contains a total of 18 songs, whereas the final single LP included only 11 tracks. Two songs found on the double package would eventually turn up on the B-sides of singles issued to help push the album.

Five tracks remain officially unreleased. They are "Mr. H Atom" and "You Know I'll Get You Baby"—a pair of new-wavish techno-rockers, the first of which features Linda on primary lead vocals. These are by far the best of the unreleased recordings. The remaining three songs which have never been issued in any official form are "All You Horseriders," "Blue Sway" and "Bogey Wobble." The latter two are instrumentals, the first a forerunner to today's New Age muzak, the second an experimental venture into "sounds" and special effects which would have been right at home on the old Zapple label. "All Your Horseriders" is an embarrassingly insipid song, with virtually spoken-word lyrics by Paul who merely shouts instructions to all of the horseriders to go ride their horses. Musically it represents an uninspired bit of synthesizer dabbling.

The eleven tracks which were eventually issued on the single album can be divided into the following categories: "Frozen Jap," "Front Parlour," "Darkroom" and "Coming Up" are all considerably longer in their original presentations and also feature noticeably different mixes. For example, "Coming Up" is more than a minute and a half longer and features additional lyrics not found on the edited release.

"Summer's Day Song" appears here strictly as an instrumental number—whereas Paul added a vocal track for the final release.

Basically unchanged are "Waterfalls," "Bogey Music," "Temporary Secretary," "On the Way," "One of These Days" and "Nobody Knows." The two tracks which found their way onto McCartney B-sides are "Check My Machine" and "Secret Friend." The former is almost a full three minutes longer on this original line-up, while the latter is actually shorter by twenty-five seconds than it appears on the UK-only 12-inch single of "Temporary Secretary." "Check My Machine" appears in a decidedly different mix and edit than can be found on the "Waterfalls single," obviously going through a severe edit and remix before being issued.

So there you have it—yet another finished but unreleased Fab-related album. This follows in the footsteps of such noted "completed-but-unreleased" album projects as McCartney's **Cold Cuts**, George Harrison's **Somewhere in England** and the Beatles' **Get Back**—all of which have eventually been issued in bootleg and/or complete counterfeit form.

Despite one's own critical assessment of these particular McCartney compositions, **The Lost McCartney Album—The Unreleased McCartney II** is a definite addition for all serious McCartney fans and collectors, serving to give further insight into the creative process involved in the record making business.

The front cover features a black and white photo of Paul which itself is an alternate shot from the same session used for the cover of the actual **McCartney II** album. Once again, Club Sandwich Records has produced an outstanding bootleg release, featuring excellent sound quality and a clean vinyl pressing.

[For the record, four of these tracks—"Mr. H Atom," "Bogey Wobble," "You Know I'll Get You Baby" and "Summer Day's Song"—were issued on the previously reviewed European bootleg **Raving On** in absolutely horrible sound quality. Unplayable in fact. And with the wrong song titles! Anyone who believes they have heard or possess these unreleased tracks based on this album, should think again. You don't.]

The Lost McCartney Album—The Unreleased McCartney II is another historic bootleg release to be gladly welcomed.

PHOTOS COURTESY OF:
Page 5—Joe Dera and Associates
Page 8—Charles F. Rosenay and Good Day Sunshine
Page 9—Horst Fascher and Good Day Sunshine:
Page 10—Joe Dera and Associates
Page 13—Bill Last
Page 16—Horst Fascher and Good Day Sunshine
Page 21— Horst Fascher and Good Day Sunshine
Page 32—Joe Dera and Associates
Page 38— Joe Sunseri and Good Day Sunshine
Page 43—Bill Last
Page 46—Charles F. Rosenay and Good Day Sunshine
Page 58—Bill Last
Page 72— Sam Leach and Good Day Sunshine
Page 81— Bill Last
Page 95— Joe Dera and Associates
Page 96—Joe Dera and Associates
Front Cover—Bill Last
Back Cover—Linda McCartney and MPL Communications Ltd.

EDWARD GROSS has written for a variety of publications, including PREMIERE, STARLOG, COMICS SCENE, NEW YORK/LONG ISLAND NIGHTLIFE, FANGORIA and CINEFANTASTIQUE. He is the author of TREK: THE LOST YEARS, THE UNOFFICIAL TALE OF BEAUTY AND THE BEAST, THE MAKING OF THE NEXT GENERATION, THE ODD COUPLE COMPANION, SECRET FILE: THE MAKING OF A WISEGUY and PAUL McCARTNEY: 20 YEARS ON HIS OWN. In addition, he co-authored the story for an episode of ABC's SUPERCARRIER and his first screenplay is scheduled to go into production later this year. He lives on Long Island, New York with his wife Eileen and their son, Teddy.

The Phantom
The Green Hornet
The Shadow
The Batman

Each issue of Serials Adventures Presents offers 100 or more pages of pure nostalgic fun for $16.95

Flash Gordon Part One
Flash Gordon Part Two
Blackhawk

Each issue of Serials Adventures Presents features a chapter by chapter review of a rare serial combined with biographies of the stars and behind-the-scenes information. Plus rare photos. See the videotapes and read the books!

THE U.N.C.L.E. TECHNICAL MANUAL

Every technical device completely detailed and blueprinted, including weapons, communications, weaponry, organization, facitilites... 80 pages, 2 volumes...$9.95 each

NUMBER SIX: THE COMPLEAT PRISONER

The most unique and intelligent television series ever aired! Patrick McGoohan's tour-de-force of spies and mental mazes finally explained episode by episode, including an interview with the McGoohan and the complete layout of the real village!...160 pages...$14.95

THE GREEN HORNET

Daring action adventure with the Green Hornet and Kato. This show appeared before Bruce Lee had achieved popularity but delivered fun, superheroic action. Episode guide and character profiles combine to tell the whole story...120 pages...$14.95

WILD, WILD, WEST

Is it a Western or a Spy show? We couldn't decide so we're listing it twice. Fantastic adventure, convoluted plots, incredible devices...all set in the wild, wild west! Details of fantastic devices, character profiles and an episode-by-episode guide...120 pages...$17.95

THE FREDDY KRUEGER STORY

The making of the monster. Including interviews with director Wes Craven and star Robert Englund. Plus an interview with Freddy himself! $14.95

THE ALIENS STORY

Interviews with movie director James Cameron, stars Sigourney Weaver and Michael Biehn and effects people and designers Ron Cobb, Syd Mead, Doug Beswick and lots more!...$14.95

ROBOCOP

Law enforcement in the future. Includes interviews with the stars, the director, the writer, the special effects people, the storyboard artists and the makeup men! $16.95

MONSTERLAND'S HORROR IN THE '80s

The definitive book of the horror films of the '80s. Includes interviews with the stars and makers of Aliens, Freddy Krueger, Robocop, Predator, Fright Night, Terminator and all the others! $17.95

LOST IN SPACE

THE COMPLEAT LOST IN SPACE
244 PAGES...$17.95
TRIBUTE BOOK
Interviews with everyone!...$7.95
TECH MANUAL
Technical diagrams to all of the special ships and devices plus exclusive production artwork....$9.95

GERRY ANDERSON

SUPERMARIONATION
Episode guides and character profiles to Capt Scarlet, Stingray, Fireball, Thunderbirds, Supercar and more...240 pages...$17.95

BEAUTY AND THE BEAST

THE UNOFFICIAL BEAUTY&BEAST
Complete first season guide including interviews and biographies of the stars. 132 pages $14.95

DARK SHADOWS

DARK SHADOWS TRIBUTE BOOK
Interviews, scripts and more... 160 pages...$14.95

DARK SHADOWS INTERVIEWS BOOK
A special book interviewing the entire cast. $18.95

DOCTOR WHO THE BAKER YEARS

A complete guide to Tom Baker's seasons as the Doctor including an in-depth episode guide, interviews with the companions and profiles of the characters... 300 pages...$19.95

THE DOCTOR WHO ENCYCLOPEDIA: THE FOURTH DOCTOR

Encyclopedia of every character, villain and monster of the Baker Years. ..240 pages...$19.95

Boring, but Necessary Ordering Information!

Payment: All orders must be prepaid by check or money order. Do not send cash. All payments must be made in US funds only.

Shipping: We offer several methods of shipment for our product.

Postage is as follows:

For books priced under $10.00— for the first book add $2.50. For each additional book under $10.00 add $1.00. (This is per individual book priced under $10.00, not the order total.)

For books priced over $10.00— for the first book add $3.25. For each additional book over $10.00 add $2.00. (This is per individual book priced over $10.00, not the order total.)

These orders are filled as quickly as possible. Sometimes a book can be delayed if we are temporarily out of stock. You should note on your order whether you prefer us to ship the book as soon as available or send you a merchandise credit good for other TV goodies or send you your money back immediately. Shipments normally take 2 or 3 weeks, but allow up to 12 weeks for delivery.

Special UPS 2 Day Blue Label RUSH SERVICE: Special service is available for desperate Couch Potatos. These books are shipped within 24 hours of when we receive your order and should take 2 days to get from us to you.

For the first **RUSH SERVICE** book under $10.00 add $4.00. For each additional 1 book under $10.00 and $1.25. (This is per individual book priced under $10.00, not the order total.)

For the first **RUSH SERVICE** book over $10.00 add $6.00. For each additional book over $10.00 add $3.50 per book. (This is per individual book priced over $10.00, not the order total.)

Canadian and Foreign shipping rates are the same except that Blue Label RUSH SERVICE is not available. All Canadian and Foreign orders are shipped as books or printed matter.

DISCOUNTS! DISCOUNTS! Because your orders are what keep us in business we offer a discount to people that buy a lot of our books as our way of saying thanks. On orders over $25.00 we give a 5% discount. On orders over $50.00 we give a 10% discount. On orders over $100.00 we give a 15% discount. On orders over $150.00 we give a 20% discount. Please list alternates when possible. Please state if you wish a refund or for us to backorder an item if it is not in stock.

100% satisfaction guaranteed. We value your support. You will receive a full refund as long as the copy of the book you are not happy with is received back by us in reasonable condition. No questions asked, except we would like to know how we failed you. Refunds and credits are given as soon as we receive back the item you do not want.

Please have mercy on Phyllis and carefully fill out this form in the neatest way you can. Remember, she has to read a lot of them every day and she wants to get it right and keep you happy! You may use a duplicate of this order blank as long as it is clear. **Please don't forget to include payment! And remember, we *love* repeat friends...**

ORDER FORM

_____ The Phantom $16.95
_____ The Green Hornet $16.95
_____ The Shadow $16.95
_____ Flash Gordon Part One $16.95 _____ Part Two $16.95
_____ Blackhawk $16.95
_____ Batman $16.95
_____ The UNCLE Technical Manual One $9.95 _____ Two $9.95
_____ The Green Hornet Television Book $14.95
_____ Number Six The Prisoner Book $14.95
_____ The Wild Wild West $17.95
_____ Trek Year One $10.95
_____ Trek Year Two $12.95
_____ Trek Year Three $12.95
_____ The Animated Trek $14.95
_____ The Movies $12.95
_____ Next Generation $19.95
_____ The Lost Years $14.95
_____ The Trek Encyclopedia $19.95
_____ Interviews Aboard The Enterprise $18.95
_____ The Ultimate Trek $75.00
_____ Trek Handbook $12.95 _____ Trek Universe $17.95
_____ The Crew Book $17.95
_____ The Making of the Next Generation $14.95
_____ The Freddy Krueger Story $14.95
_____ The Aliens Story $14.95
_____ Robocop $16.95
_____ Monsterland's Horror in the '80s $17.95
_____ The Compleat Lost in Space $17.95
_____ Lost in Space Tribute Book $9.95
_____ Lost in Space Tech Manual $9.95
_____ Supermarionation $17.95
_____ The Unofficial Beauty and the Beast $14.95
_____ Dark Shadows Tribute Book $14.95
_____ Dark Shadows Interview Book $18.95
_____ Doctor Who Baker Years $19.95
_____ The Doctor Who Encyclopedia: The 4th Doctor $19.95
_____ Illustrated Stephen King $12.95
_____ Gunsmoke Years $14.95

NAME:_____

STREET:_____

CITY:_____

STATE:_____

ZIP:_____

TOTAL:_____ SHIPPING_____

SEND TO: COUCH POTATO, INC.
5715 N BALSAM, LAS VEGAS, NV 89130